THE "IDEAL" COUPLE

THE "IDEAL" COUPLE

The Shadow Side of a Marriage

Marilyn J. Minter Wolgemuth and J. Carl Wolgemuth

with
Laurie Oswald Robinson

Foreword by
Ann Showalter

DreamSeeker Books
TELFORD, PENNSYLVANIA

an imprint of
Cascadia Publishing House

Cascadia Publishing House orders, information, reprint permissions:
contact@CascadiaPublishingHouse.com
1-215-723-9125
126 Klingerman Road, Telford PA 18969
www.CascadiaPublishingHouse.com

The "Ideal" Couple
Copyright © 2011 by Cascadia Publishing House LLC
Telford, PA 18969
All rights reserved
DreamSeeker Books is an imprint of Cascadia Publishing House LLC
Library of Congress Catalog Number: 2011007370
ISBN 13: 978-1-931038-86-7; **ISBN 10:** 1-931038-86-4
Book design by Cascadia Publishing House
Cover design by Gwen M. Stamm

All Bible quotations are used by permission, all rights reserved and, unless otherwise noted, are from *The New Revised Standard Version of the Bible*, copyright 1989, by the Division of Christian Education of the National Council of the Churches of Christ in the USA.

Library of Congress Cataloguing-in-Publication Data
Wolgemuth, Marilyn J. Minter, 1930-
  The "ideal" couple : the shadow side of a marriage / Marilyn J. Minter Wolgemuth and J. Carl Wolgemuth with Laurie Oswald Robinson.
    p. cm.
  Includes bibliographical references (p.   ).
  ISBN-13: 978-1-931038-86-7 (trade pbk. : alk. paper)
  ISBN-10: 1-931038-86-4 (trade pbk. : alk. paper)
  1. Wolgemuth, Marilyn J. Minter, 1930---Marriage. 2. Wolgemuth, Carl--Marriage. 3. Mennonites--United States--Biography. 4. Christian gays--United States--Biography. I. Wolgemuth, Carl. II. Robinson, Laurie Oswald. III. Title.
BX8143.W65A3 2011
289.7092'2--dc22
[B]

                                    2011007370

20 19 18 17 16 15 14 13 12 11   10 9 8 7 6 5 4 3 2 1

Dedication

To my two dear friends who have been my Lifeline:

Beverly,
*who has journeyed with me over the years giving me much
needed support
when I couldn't even pray;*

Judy,
*who listens to me when I am hurting, has stood by me over
these many years,
and picked me up when I fell into despair.*

MJW

Contents

Foreword

Marilyn and J. Carl Wolgemuth developed a friendship that led in due time to the day of their wedding, where standing before a pastor, their families, and a faith community they pledged faithfulness to each other no matter what the future might hold. Like most couples who are committed to following Christ, they must have hoped to build a strong, loving family in the years to ahead. However, lurking in the background that day was a secret that Carl had chosen not to reveal to Marilyn: He lived with a powerful attraction to men.

On one hand Carl's choice to keep his secret is understandable since in 1955, the year they were married, no one in the church or in society was speaking openly about same-sex attraction. Young men caught in the bind Carl found himself in felt they had no option except to marry a woman, often with the hope that their attraction for men might thus be solved. Furthermore, there is little, if anything, that carries the burden of stigma and shame associated with same-sex attraction.

At the same time keeping his secret was destined to result in a complex marriage relationship he could not have foreseen or imagined. Eventually his secret could not be kept; it had to be faced within the marriage. For a wife to discover that the man she married would much prefer to be intimate with a man than with her is devastating to say the least. That discovery undermines her sense of self, her self confidence, her femininity, and her trust in her husband, leaving her with a host of questions and confusion and sometimes a slowly simmering anger.

On the surface the Wolgemuths maintained the appearance of a normal couple while internally both were deeply wounded. The relationship was stressed by separation, secrecy, and homosexual infidelity and repeated disappointments. They spent many sessions in marriage counseling, but despite all the effort, it seemed little changed. Yet they persevered because they considered the sacredness of their vows.

It is quite amazing that amid severe pain and chaos both Carl and Marilyn spent most of their lives in Christian ministry. Marilyn pursued her entire fifty-nine years as a nurse in various settings, including working in remote villages in Mexico where she, her husband, and their daughter worked among the Isthmus Aztec Indian ethnic group under Wycliffe Bible Translators. Following her years in Mexico, Marilyn spent fifteen years in psychiatric nursing in Texas and Kansas.

During their years of service in Mexico, Carl was not only a linguist/translator but also spent seven years at Wycliffe's International Center where he became proficient in computer-assisted typesetting New Testaments. Carl completed a Master's degree at age sixty-three and taught linguistics until his retirement.

The Wolgemth's story is both tragedy and blessing, suffering and commitment, mercy and grace. It is one more example of the depths of God's unchanging love for people who seek to follow him even though they sometimes have difficulty loving themselves or each other.

—*Ann Showalter*
  Wichita, Kansas
  Author, Touched by Grace: From Secrecy to New Life

Authors' Preface

Through the years, people have told us we looked like an "ideal couple." Down deep inside we knew we were far from that image—we were just good at pretending everything was fine. Recently we both concluded that keeping up an appearance of the ideal couple was not the right thing to do so we agreed to strip the pretenses, the hypocrisy and become more authentic. We will put the ideal couple illusion to rest by writing this memoir and let the chips fall where they may.

Our story begins with our growing up in the 1930s in religious, fundamentalist environments that included abandonment, emotional abuses, silence, and fear. As two wounded souls, we developed a friendship, got married, and, through sheer determination struggled to maintain an unusual marital relationship punctuated by betrayal, sexual infidelity, and bisexuality.

Writing intimately about our troubled marriage has been like the pangs of childbirth—some tears, some laughter, an emotional and labor-intensive project. By being candid and straightforward in sharing the marital stresses that for so long we minimized or denied and hid from others, we trust that God's healing light will be shed more broadly among our Christian communities on topics that are often closeted into powerful and destructive secrets. We are aware our story may trigger a reader's own unpleasant, repressed memories. Uncovered pain can be a blessing in disguise if it nudges a person toward seeking needed help. If our story evokes a strong reaction, we encourage readers to connect with a trusted pastor, friend, or therapist.

When we first started writing, we used pseudonyms instead of our real names mainly due to fear of rejection by our friends and family if they knew what our struggles have been. However, after reading Elyn Saks' autobiography, *The Center Cannot Hold: My Journey into Madness,* we took courage from this paragraph:

> My experience of revealing my illness to all these people has been eye-opening. Most have been very accepting; many said they had no idea and were shocked. . . . A psychiatrist urged me to use a nom de plume (pen name, pseudonym) when writing this book, but I thought that would send the wrong message—that all of this was too awful to say out loud (and let everybody know it is me). Ultimately, I decided that writing about myself could do more good than any academic article I'd ever pen. Why do it under a pseudonym if what I intended was to tell the truth? I don't want to be marginalized; I've fought against that all my life.

As we discussed how best to share our journey, the question arose: for whom are we writing this memoir? The answer was always the same: primarily for anyone who is tempted to give up the struggles in a difficult relationship. A secondary reason was to help readers who are in a more stable relationship to better understand the inner turmoil involved in a troubled marriage. The details of our story are woven together using a dialogue format that identifies each of us. They are gleaned from our reflections, diaries, journals, and letters written over a period of years. We chose examples that best portrayed the painful process of seeking answers to our inner conflicts, with a look at the bigger picture.

Despite the pain of the telling and the reading, we take this risk of opening up ourselves for redemptive purposes. It's our prayer that the chronicle of our journey will show that it is possible for a couple to stay together even against all odds. Divorce isn't the only response to a seemingly intolerable life situation. God's grace can transcend difficulties but it requires some sacrifice, transparency and willingness to change. This is a testimony to God's faithful, patient work in our lives and hopefully will be an encouragement for others to work on the tough problems even if it's tempting to give up. We experience awe and wonder as we reflect on how God has used our sincere efforts to seek his will and serve him despite hurt and disillusionment. We give him credit for any accomplishments we've achieved as well as the perseverance to remain in a deeply flawed marriage.

Touched by God's grace we work toward accepting each other as we are, not as we wish the other would be. We do this fallibly—one acquaintance reading a prepublication copy of the book observed how easily in a marriage in which one partner struggles with same-sex attractions the other spouse may be viewed as the one more sinned against than sinning, for example, and that is no doubt a risk here. We also recognize that readers will vary in their understandings of what healing should look like in a marriage faced with such circumstances as ours.

Yet we pray that grace has helped us come out of the false light of the "ideal" and has enabled us to believe the light of God's love can illuminate all our human shadows, empowering us to face them and not to run away in fear. In that spirit, we invite our readers to enter this story, filled with the grace of God that may give hope to others whose lives are dappled with shadows, sunlight and the eye of God that touches all with a loving and healing gaze.

—*Carl and Marilyn Wolgemuth*

Acknowledgments

Many people have had a part in shaping who we are as individuals and as a couple today.

We honor our parents, now gone on to their reward. They did the best they knew how in showing us the way to live life.

Friends too numerous to mention have given of themselves through prayer to encourage us along the way.

Many therapists, counselors, pastors, and psychiatrists have done what they could to help us deal realistically with our particular set of problems and character traits.

Thanks to our friends and family who read the manuscript, shared constructive feedback, and gave their support to our project.

To Dick and Mary Rempel, retired publisher and editor, we give our thanks for consenting to read the manuscript, make suggestions, and gently guide us through the maze of details that go with publication.

And finally, our sincere thanks go to Laurie Oswald Robinson, who faithfully did professional editing of the manuscript before submission to the publisher. She did an exceptional job of arranging our original writings into an easier-to-follow format. Our work together has resulted in a valued friendship.

Thank you, Laurie.

THE "IDEAL" COUPLE

Chapter One

The Early Years

MARILYN

1930-1948

I was born on a Kansas farm in 1930, the only child of my birth mother, who died of a ruptured appendix when I was barely three. I don't remember her at all except for pictures and what other people have told me about her. Her friends told me that I was a lot like her—musical and fun-loving. What feelings did I experience when I no longer had a mother? I have no idea. My two grandmothers, Emma and Nancy, stepped in to care for me, so I can't say I felt unloved or completely abandoned, but I'm sure a toddler must have experienced a plethora of feelings.

What kind of nurturing had my mother given me in those three years? She herself did not have the best model for mothering. This is how the sketchy story has been passed on to me: My grandfather left the family after my mother was born. My grandmother Nancy put my mother (age four) and her older brother (ten) in a church-sponsored orphanage in Oklahoma. After that, grandmother Nancy—"the wild one" as her family called her—married and divorced three more times. When my mother was ready for high school, the orphanage sent her to our church school in Upland, California. That is where she met Dad, who was in his senior year. It's interesting that Dad sent me to this same school for my own senior year in high school.

I have clear memories of when I was four years old being sexually molested for a short time by a sixteen-year-old old hired man. My dad found out and promptly fired him. These experiences impacted my life in subtle ways but, years later, I worked through both traumas with the help of a therapist.

Dad remarried eighteen months later, and my sister and two brothers were born. My stepmother was attentive to me during the first year until she had her own children, then it seemed like she preferred them to me. When she became moody she would not speak to me for several days at a time. The tension was almost palpable. I wondered, *What did I do to displease her?* Thus I learned to be a people-pleaser at a young age.

As a stepchild, I often felt like an orphan must feel, like I didn't really fit in this family and had to be careful not to make her unhappy. I wanted so much for her to accept me. After I was an adult, she admitted to me that she was jealous of me as the child of Dad's first wife. That helped me understand a bit better why we didn't get along very well.

Our home was a "religioholic" one. Conformity in plain dress and behavior, the rule of the small faith community, was emphasized to the exclusion of the person as an individual. Three times a year, for two or three weeks, an itinerant preacher held revivals that were designed for confessing all the transgressions that were committed since the last revival. At age five, I asked Jesus to come into my heart and from then on church people nurtured me in the Christian faith. But my vivacious personality created a problem for the stern, staid, and sedate church people at the small country church where we attended!

Since my father was a deacon, he was very strict with us children. It would reflect on his parenting if any of us deviated from the straight and narrow! He believed in spanking, and I received many due to my mischievous nature. One spanking I clearly remember when I was around age five. During a Wednesday night prayer meeting, I turned around and stuck my tongue out at the persons sitting behind me. My father took me outside in the cold winter air to deliver a heavy-handed spanking. He ended with, "Now tell Daddy you love me." What a confusing message! Other spankings came after I had been potty-trained but would still wet the bed at night. When spanking didn't stop the wetting, they took me to a clinic to see if something was physically wrong. There wasn't. To this day, I believe it was reaction against all the emotional upheavals in my life.

My first six years on the farm were the Depression years: 1930-1936. We lived very simply, growing and processing most of our own food. Mom made plain dresses for my sister and me out of the colorful flour and sugar sacks, some with dainty flower patterns, others with bold plaids or stripes. We had little money for extras during those years, but I recall Dad being a diligent money-manager and have managed my own financial matters by his example. It was enjoyable following Dad around the farm, and as a teenager, I did a lot of the field work with him. My parents were also very hospitable and regularly entertained guests at our dinner table. My interest in missions was generated mainly from the many stories that missionaries told us when we hosted them in our home.

Through rain, snow or sleet, drought, or mud, I walked a mile to the one-room school for the elementary grades. I rode the bus ten miles to high school. School was a highlight of my early years. It was where I felt accepted, made good grades, excelled in music, athletics, and dramatic readings.

By fifteen, I desperately tried to persuade Dad to tell me more about my birth mother and her extended family. He either didn't know much himself or was unwilling to give me any information, fearing it would hurt Mom's feelings if he talked about his first wife. This led me to believe that there must be some deep, dark, hidden secret about my heritage. I attempted to run away from home to live with my maternal grandmother in western Kansas, hoping that my intense longing, this quest to find out more about my mother, could be satisfied. My plan was abruptly aborted, however, and I never tried it again.

As a teenager, I was unhappy and confused about spiritual things to the degree that I rebelled mostly against the arbitrary conformist rules and regulations of the church, but also against my parents' attitudes. In high school my girlfriends and I stood out like sore thumbs because we wore our head coverings and "plain" clothes. Young people in our church couldn't go to movies, ball games, drama productions, or other "worldly" activities.

At school, I hung out with some of the girls who wore make-up and read trashy love-story magazines. At my request, they would loan me some of these True Love magazines and I hid them under my mattress at home to read later, trying to get a sense of what "true love" was all about. I know now it was not an accurate depiction of love, but it fostered an idealistic "love" which I carried into my expectations of marriage.

My parents wouldn't allow me to date while I lived at home. But when I went away to church boarding school for my senior year in high school, I had my first date experience.

I remember how countrified and awkward I felt with this college freshman guy who seemed so sophisticated.

CARL

I was born in 1931, the oldest of three, at home in a small town, Florin, Pennsylvania, which is now Mount Joy. My older sister was six years younger and my younger sister was adopted when I was nineteen years old. Mother wasn't well during the first year or two after I was born. I was told she had a hard labor with me and took a long time to heal after giving birth. Dad's sister Grace, a registered nurse, came and took care of me in those early days.

Dad often told me that I was a sickly child with frequent severe ear infections. I was hospitalized for two days in May 1935 with mastoiditis when I was only three-and-a-half years old. I remember how abandoned I felt. I cried and cried when Mommy and Daddy weren't around. I can still see the night nurse with her slipper-like cap perched on the back of her head, coming into the ward and sternly telling me to stop crying. I did.

Also as a child, I was subject to convulsions. My parents went to the Chicago World's Fair in 1933, leaving me with Auntie and Uncle. Much to Auntie's consternation, I spiked a fever and went into convulsions. As she held me, she recounts, my body stiffened and my eyes rolled up till only the whites showed. She said she gave me a cool enema to bring down my fever. Somehow I survived.

When I didn't have a bowel movement often enough to suit my mother, she would give me an enema. I always felt violated by this procedure, but it was interesting to see the little marbles that came out. With all that attention to my bottom, I thought it would be all right to show it off, so I often took all my clothes off and ran around the house naked, much to Mother's dismay.

I was a very serious, shy, introverted, studious, quiet young man—a loner who never could fit in with my peers on sports. I was awkward and couldn't throw a ball straight or run in relays. I was the last one to be chosen on a team which only accentuated my aloneness.

Our family dynamics were a confusing, mixed bag. We had some good times together, like picnics and travel. But not all was fun and games. Mom and Dad would often go for days without speaking to each other or me. I didn't like women in general, including my mother, especially if they didn't fit my ideal body image. In fact, I had even hated my female teachers in grade school. I resented my father, too, for the harsh discipline he administered for minor infractions. There were times when I was afraid of Dad and didn't want to be alone with him. I was often scolded and punished for saying or doing something that would embarrass Dad. Sometimes I didn't know what I had done wrong. He kept a razor strap on a nail on the door casing outside the bathroom. He would use the strap on my bare bottom when he thought I needed it. When I talked with Aunt Esther in later years about those days, she said, "Your daddy was pretty hard on you, and I could hardly stand it sometimes."

I did not like my father very much. At one time I vowed that I didn't want to be like him. One memory of my early years was a framed piece of needlework that hung on the wall of my bedroom, probably a family heirloom. On it was this cryptic embroidered four-word message: "To my dear father." I often looked at that phrase and tried to think up hateful words to put in place of "dear." Strangely, now I don't remember what any of those words were.

I was thirteen when Dad, at age thirty-nine, had his spiritual awakening during the spring revival of 1944. To my surprise, Dad said to me one evening before the service, "Son, if you have a desire to make a start, I'd encourage you to go up to the altar when the invitation is given." I went forward that night and accepted Christ as my savior. After much prayer and tears, I had that "born again" experience that we were taught to expect. I had a strong assurance of sins forgiven and God's acceptance. That meant so much to me as one who often felt misunderstood and rejected. I had a taste of exquisite joy and was absolutely euphoric.

But an emotional high has to come down, and it wasn't long before I wondered how to get it back. That is one of the problems I have with a revivalistic approach to spiritual life. Revivalism is often offered as a quick fix for dealing with complex emotional issues.

Mother never talked about spiritual things except on rare occasions during testimony time at church. I can remember her using the biblical phrase "peace which passeth all understanding." To my young ears, the first three words of that phrase came out something like "peach with patches." But seriously, it seemed so out of character for her to talk about faith in her self-conscious way that I felt very uncomfortable when she did.

Dad, on the other hand, often spoke authoritatively of spiritual things. He would invariably quote Scripture in such a way that there was no room to raise questions, since that would be questioning the Scriptures. Sometimes it felt as though he was using the Bible as a club over my head.

My personal style was shaped by both my parents. I rejected Dad's style of making pronouncements about spiritual things, and picked up Mom's reticence to speak of personal faith matters. By the time I was an adult I was terribly ambivalent about God.

Plenty of Scripture reinforced that sense of low self-worth, of non-being. Jesus is reported to have said, "Apart from me you can do nothing." Also, Paul wrote, "I know that in me, that is in my flesh, dwells no good thing." The Old Testament is quoted in the New: "There is none righteous, no not one." Other horrendous truths were part of what I heard as a child: "All liars shall have their part in the lake of fire." "Our righteousness is as filthy rags." "It is better to enter life maimed than with two feet and to be cast into hell." "God punishes us for our own good."

I took it all so literally. Yet, as an adult, I chose to be a missionary Bible translator. Guess what the hardest part about that was? How church leaders in the indigenous culture used the Bible to feed their own dysfunction.

In retrospect, I see the religious faith I grew up with as a toxic influence in my life. My family of origin was dysfunctional in significant ways. I don't know how much the religion was responsible for the family dysfunction. Maybe our family simply keyed into the aspects of religion that fed the dysfunction, but whichever way it was, there was shame and guilt aplenty.

There were *shoulds* that never got carried out: We *should* witness more, we *should* pray more, we *should* be joyful, we *should* tithe, we *should* all go to prayer meeting. Not fulfilling all those obligations left me riddled with guilt and in doubt of my self-worth. I figured that, apart from a right standing with God, I was nothing but lost.

My thirteenth birthday was special for me. It meant I was a *teenager*—no longer a little kid. Now we were getting somewhere. As a child, I often felt powerless and put upon by the two adults who ruled my life. Deep inside I was a rebel. Many times I thought about running away from home but never could figure out where to go. As a young child, I remember thinking: *I've been a child my whole life, and I guess I always will be.* But now, in reaching the magic thirteen, I could see that there was hope. I wouldn't be a child forever. I would eventually escape the galling dependency that was my experience of being a child. Then I would have some say-so in my life.

When I was fifteen, I became infatuated with a thirteen year old neighbor boy. That was an awesome awakening of my sexuality and was a precursor for my growing desire for intimacy with males and having an attitude of contempt for females the rest of my life.

2

Meeting in College
September 1948—May 1950

CARL

In September 1948, I enrolled as an Academy Senior in our church's small denominational school, Messiah Academy and two-year Junior College, in Pennsylvania with a total of 200 students. I noticed Marilyn on the first day of school. Her hair was dark brown, and the part of her hair that showed in front of her white head covering was combed in a gentle wave. Her purposeful walk gave the impression that she was all business. I also was impressed that she was a piano player, and often practiced on the piano in the student lounge.

One day not long after school started, Marilyn was playing the last measures of Paderewski's *Minuet*. The silvery strains of music wafted out the open windows could be heard over the campus. As I walked into the lounge, she got up from the piano and headed for the door. I wanted to let her know that I enjoyed her playing, so I said, "There's my girl!" She walked right by me and out the door. Had she not heard me? Or did she hear and not like what I said?

I loved music, so over the next five years at Messiah I became part of the male chorus, a mixed quartet, and oratorio chorus. I also took voice lessons. Guess who my accompanist turned out to be—Marilyn. I felt so fortunate. She played well for my selection of songs: *O, Lord Most Holy* (Panis Angelicus), *My Task* (To love someone more dearly every day), and *If I Have Wounded Any Soul Today*.

The gospel team organization was an important part of student activities. Interested students were assigned in teams of two as co-chairpersons to plan programs. Each team was to select other students to volunteer for Sunday night inspirational programs in local churches or the inner city rescue mission. My first year I was not involved in gospel team. Marilyn had been assigned to work with Paul, president of the student body. I thought that to be linked up with him was to be in a position of great esteem. My second year, Marilyn and I were assigned to be gospel team co-chairs. That was a pleasant surprise to me.

I chose the field of religious education to study in college. I wanted to be thought of as spiritual so I was faithful to the denomination's dress code by wearing suit coats with a clergy-type collar and parted my hair in the middle. The church fathers frowned on neckties for men. So if I didn't wear my clerical coat, I buttoned my shirt clear up to the neck and wore it without a necktie.

During my freshman year Rachel, a girl from my hometown, and I regularly chatted in the lounge as good friends. I told her that if there was a school function and she had no date, I would be her date. Then, I began to think about dating other girls. For one of the first school functions I asked another girl to go with me. Rachel was left to wonder what had happened and became tearful. That lack of understanding on my part was very unfair to her. The next day I apologized to her for not making it clear that I wanted to be free to date other girls.

I recount this part of my story because of how it reveals a certain disdain and lack of sensitivity in my relationships with women. At some level, I knew I had an aversion to women and so the few dating experiences I had in college were steeped in ambivalence.

MARILYN

In those days, for a woman to go to college was equivalent to husband hunting so I wondered if I would find one. For spending money, at fifty cents an hour, I agreed to accompany several voice students, one of them was Carl. I noticed he carefully avoided being too close to me. He was so shy that he would stand at the farthest end of the student lounge and listen to me play Beethoven's *Sonata Pathetique* on the piano

I also conscientiously conformed to our denomination's stringent, conservative plain dress code. I wore the traditional white head covering and cape dresses. My long dark brown hair was twisted up into a bun under the covering. This was expected of the women at that time. If we dressed otherwise, our entire spirituality would be questioned. We would be considered worldly and expected to give account for it.

My sophomore year, Carl and I were assigned as co-leaders to the inner-city church, The Lighthouse Chapel, where several of us gave a monthly evening church service. As we planned the programs, we discovered we had several interests in common: music, art, missions, and nature. By springtime, we had developed a very special interest in each other that went beyond planning programs. The wooded Minnemingo trail on campus beckoned us to enjoy the fragrance of emerging flowers and leafing trees, so this "budding" couple would sometimes go there to plan our programs.

Being the romantic type, I was smitten and would secretly watch this quiet, tall, dark-haired, and handsome guy as he waited on tables in the student dining room. However, we both knew the gospel team policy—no dating. Toward the end of the spring semester, most of the students knew we were out on the trail at times other than when we were planning programs. After our last gospel team program, a couple of my friends encouraged Carl to ask me for a date before the end of the school year.

He was so shy that everyone was surprised when he actually did! He waited for me by the women's coat room and hesitantly asked me to go to the class night program with him. I was thrilled. Afterward, we strolled down to the ice cream parlor at the bottom of the hill and chatted for awhile—a very quiet, unpretentious time together—no bells or whistles.

Two days later, in May 1950, after my tough pre-nursing and math courses were over, I graduated with a two-year associate degree. By then Messiah had become an accredited four-year college so Carl continued his study program there for three more years. In September I headed to Lancaster General Hospital for three years of nursing school.

3

Our Courtship Years
May 1950–March 1954

MARILYN

During the summer between my graduation and nursing school we dated about every other week. I soon realized that my feelings for him were stronger than his feelings were for me. I was naive and missed seeing a lot of the warning signs: *Me:* "He needs me to speak for him." *He:* "She's a nurse, she can take care of me. I'm socially inept."

He was often preoccupied with his own thoughts, which made for awkward conversation. It was hard to know where our relationship was going. This early in our relationship, I didn't want to assume anything. Did he consider that we were going steady or just good friends? I was taught that the man initiates everything and the woman is to be a submissive follower. I struggled. Would I be too forward if I brought it up?

Two months after we started dating I wrote a letter to him reporting that

> *it would be better if we didn't see each other anymore unless we have an understanding of how we both view the relationship. We've been good friends and I've appreciated your friendship but as far as dating is concerned, I don't want to lead you on, and neither do I want you to lead me on. I don't want to take things for granted. . . . I need to know what's in your thinking. . . .*

When I think of all the fun our gang had on Sunday I tingle with pleasure, but also with that memory comes just a tinge of condemnation. I believe in having a good time and letting off energy that has accumulated during the week, but somehow I think we carried it just a bit far, forgetting that after all it was Sunday. After ten days of hospital duty the relaxation of being with my friends was a welcome change. I'm not usually so foolish, but when my day off comes around, I seem to pull out all the stops and have a good time. I went to Roxbury with the antici-pation of receiving spiritual food but when it's over, what is uppermost in my mind? The good sermons and uplift-ing singing? OR the mountain rides and picnic lunches?? I think I'd better take stock of myself for I fear the latter predominates!!

CARL

As you intimated in your last letter, we'll want to have the right things uppermost in our minds, so we have no need of regret. I'm trying to guard against being too silly, and my responsibilities here at the college are helping me to do that. But you know how invigorating a good laugh is once in a while.

It doesn't do half as much good, though, as last night's prayer meeting when we go in the right spirit. This morn-ing in Ethics we talked about Spencer's philosophy of the full and meaningful life. I am finding an abundance of life and joy in my Lord.

I thought of the poem,

> *Morning skies! Sunrise! Lakes and rushing waters!*
> *Make all things unlovely from my soul depart.*
> *Purple mountains rising high! Trees against the sky!*
> *Life is beautiful because God lives within my heart!*

*Oh, Marilyn, I'm praying that you and I and every one
of God's people will keep on fire or get on fire with this
thing called soul-winning. I believe we both need special
grace from the Lord to keep up that "river of living water"
that people around us are so thirsty for.*

These letters illustrate just how focused we were on serious
subjects. Carl continued with his college study program, and
when he could get free of his studies and extracurricular activities, he drove his trusty blue and white 1947 Chevy named
"Lulabelle" to pick me up at my nurses' residence. As time went
on, his letters reflected a warmer tone. He even addressed me as
sweetheart and signed them "with love." I welcomed his expres-
sions of affection, thinking he meant them the same way I was
hearing them.

During one visit to his parents' home, we made sand-
wiches, drank tea, ate fresh apricots, and talked about how
much fun it would be to look at each other across the table for
the rest of our lives. I later wrote in my journal, "Won't that be
next to paradise to live together, eat together, play together
every day instead of just once or twice a month?!"

Since movies, ball games, and any other worldly pastimes
were frowned on by church leaders, we didn't have many activities to choose from. On our dates, we attended one of the
many revival meetings at various churches in the area. Sometimes we double-dated with another couple, went to concerts,
and participated in Youth For Christ meetings. Or we sat and
talked in the car in front of the nurses' residence, with space between us, of course. We sometimes went to his parents' home
for a meal or to hang out. I felt comfortable with his parents and
felt they readily accepted me.

Having been sheltered up to this point within the confines
of the church traditions, nursing school was an eye-opener for
me. I made friends with other women my age who were Christians but they didn't have to dress the same way I did. I questioned the strict dress code imposed upon us as young people,

even though it was based on biblical principles. It was a tactic to insulate and isolate us from the real world. I believe our church leaders sadly lacked understanding of human personality. They took the Scriptures much too literally and lumped everyone together under the same rigid rules. I don't blame our church-fathers—they were only doing what they thought was right. They didn't intend it as spiritual abuse or toxic faith, but I believe that is what it was.

During my second year in nursing school, I cut my long hair, got a permanent and dressed like any ordinary person. Carl, as usual, kept his thoughts to himself but let me know in subtle ways that I was going against church tradition and being a rebel while he kept trying so hard to conform to it. Little did I know that he had struggles of a very different nature.

Toward the end of our second year of dating, I sensed a growing tension from him when his letters became fewer and farther between. I wrote and asked him to explain:

> *Carl, you may as well tell me what has come between us— I've sensed for some time that there's something wrong but I can't decide if it's my imagination or if I'm just not aware of what the tension is about. If it's something I've done or said, please tell me. If it's a growing indifference on your part, please tell me that, too. . . . Of course, I have no way of knowing whether or not you still love me like you've said before . . . Perhaps, being a girl, I feel this more deeply than you do . . . If I have said too much, forgive me. Please don't be mad at me. Love, Marilyn*

When he did not reply, I feared he wanted to end our relationship. The next time I had a couple of days off, I went to see him at the college. That's when he told me he had decided to abruptly cut me out of his life but didn't have the courage to tell me.

I shared my inner turmoil in many journal entries. Here are a couple examples:

We went for a walk on the trail to the little wooden bench fastened between two trees. The honeysuckle vines were blooming profusely and gave off their exotic fragrance. There, in that idyllic setting he talked about needing a spiritual revival and feels his soul is terribly lean . . . As far as I or anyone else could tell, he was a devout and faithful model of what a Christian should be.

He said he is very confused about our relationship and doesn't think he actually loves me or that we'd be good as life companions . . . He said he was sorry for hurting me. His being sorry didn't help me. Oh, diary, what a crushing blow! But God will strengthen me. He'll stand by me faithfully.

A few nights later: On Friday night, a great loneliness, hunger and sadness came over me like a cloud that I couldn't shake off. When I knelt to pray, the vision of our parting came over me with such force and reality that I couldn't help crying hysterically for a long time. Even though it's only been a couple of months, it seems like a year has passed that I've seen or been with him and the time is going so slow. I just want to talk to him again. It's wonderful to trust God, but I don't do it well enough . . . "My thoughts are not your thoughts, neither are my ways your ways, thus saith the Lord."

Two weeks later: We drove to Musser Park, our favorite retreat. He said these last two months were hard on him, too. I could have cried for happiness! We renewed our love for each other. It's impossible to tell all that we talked about. All I know is that we are surer than ever that we are meant for each other. It felt like a 10-ton load of bricks was lifted off of me. He reported that he is happier than he has been for months, too. He still is unsure if his love is deep enough and of the right kind. I have faith that it is and he just doesn't realize it.

Now, as I look back on this episode, lots of questions come to mind. What was I thinking when I wrote that? Did I think I could control his feelings? Was I under the illusion that I could change him? Was I in denial? Reading into his words something that wasn't there? Was I so relieved to be back in relationship that I was overly optimistic? Was I so naive and eager to take up where we left off that I didn't question whether he had resolved his earlier doubts? The answer to all these questions is YES.

I admit to being the dominant person in this relationship. My training as a nurse provided ample opportunities to thoroughly develop the characteristic of taking charge. Coupled with his passivity and ambivalence, Carl seemed perfectly willing for me to do that! For the next year, we began dating again, and our relationship was on a relatively stronger basis. He began signing his letters with . . . "Love, Carl."

Despite being together again, a tiny seed of distrust had been planted during those two months of separation. But during the next year, as we were both totally immersed in our studies, there wasn't much time to reflect. He studied furiously at college, and I slogged through my last year of nursing school. My schedule was so erratic that I occasionally had to cancel a date.

CARL

I enjoyed being with my male buddies, the international students especially, more than I enjoyed being with Marilyn. This confused me a lot and was part of the reason I broke up with her. I felt terrible for giving her so much grief. Another factor was that I was physically and spiritually exhausted from over-functioning as editor of the college yearbook and probably wasn't able to think rationally.

At one point, I wrote Marilyn a letter, attempting to "normalize" our break up and to quiet my inner turmoil:

Dear Marilyn, I think we'll be able to go along together again as though nothing ever happened. It's easy to get in the swing of something we've been accustomed to for nearly two years, is it? Yet, for myself, I feel that it's a slightly different swing, a better one in many respects. . . .

But the turmoil continued. I wrote in my journal the day I graduated from college on May 16, 1953:

Today my reflections and doubts are so puzzling to me as I contemplate my future relationship with Marilyn. Where is my life headed? What vivid memories will this present day hold—the comparative keenness of today against that of childhood? Will these days with Marilyn be like a book that's read and stored away in a dusty corner? Or will they be like a chapter in a volume ever growing, ever at the fingertips of recollection? Why can't I seem to plan my life in terms of two? Where are the fond prospects, the eagerness with which a lover ought to think of being with her, with her, with her? I must confess the days and months and years we've been together haven't brought a speck more feeling of togetherness for me, save for the fitful flutters of the heart that are dependent on my moods and just as changeable.

My Lord, to what avail has been this courtship and the times when we were sure that God was working things out for us to be together? Or maybe that nasty little shade of doubt has plagued me for a purpose. It must be gone! Or let the shade envelop the dusty book that has no reason for continuance. Right now I wish I could get away.

Those feelings of wanting to run were not only born out of my inner turmoil regarding Marilyn. They were also piqued by a traumatic experience that became a secret I clung to for many years, and didn't even share with her.

Since I was in college during the Korean War, I was classified 2-D with the draft board. This meant I was deferred from military service while studying for the ministry. Several weeks before graduation, I informed the draft board that I wanted to register as a Conscientious Objector. I would then be classified 1-W and work under the auspices of the Mennonite Central Committee (MCC) in lieu of military service. I had in mind to do what many of the 1-W men chose to do—work as a state hospital psychiatric aide.

A letter soon came from the draft board ordering me to appear for mandatory induction. This included a physical and a written psychological examination. One of the questions on the psychological examination was: "Have you ever had homosexual thoughts or tendencies?" I answered honestly—"Yes."

When the exams were reviewed, I was pulled aside and directed to see a psychiatrist. He asked lots of questions about my family: what kinds of things upset me, when was the last time I cried and what was the occasion, how I got along with my parents, how they got along with each other. Fresh in my memory was a conflict between my mother and father at the kitchen table, when I became upset enough to go to my room and cry.

After that encounter with the psychiatrist, I received a letter from Selective Service Board 83 that told me I was classified 4-F, which meant "disabled" and rejected for service. It read: "Not acceptable for induction. This person has a life-long pattern of over-dependency accompanied by almost complete and compulsively maintained restriction on aggression; bed-wetting until 17 years old; uncomfortable in groups; preoccupied at times with immature sexual fantasies; seeks and finds partial relief in religious experiences." Per Dr. Paul F. Dunn.

When I received this rejection letter I felt total panic! What should I do now? I could get a job or go back to school because with a 4-F classification I was no longer eligible for the draft. Now this was a dilemma for me. I had already signed up to do alternate service, so I had to make a choice. Since I had informed friends and family what I planned to do as a I-W, I would have to give a reason why I was changing course. I felt shame at being labeled emotionally unfit. It took me back to times when, as a child, I would be called a "sissy" for not wanting to fight.

I requested a follow-up appointment with Dr. Dunn, and he agreed to see me. I desperately wanted him to change his mind about my classification so I told him that those homosexual tendencies were a thing of the past, and I no longer had them. He didn't buy my plea. I was really uptight when he asked me several questions that were very difficult to answer. He observed that I seemed confused. I remember saying, "I'm not confused!"

The "immature sexual fantasies" part, Dr. Dunn explained, was code for homosexual inclinations. Everyone in the counseling profession would know what that means. He explained that the 4-F classification was for my protection. I would be open to harassment in the military because, as he described it, I had a total inhibition of aggression.

In contrast to my honest answer to the exam question, I did not do the most honest thing—admit to my friends and family that I was rejected and classified 4-F. Instead, I chose to hide that part of me and, from then on, the course of my life was set, based on a lie.

I reluctantly told Marilyn only part of the reason I was rejected—emotionally immature and too religious. So how could this be the problem? I was a dedicated Christian, wasn't I—after all, hadn't I just graduated with a bachelor's degree in religious education? Added to this hypocrisy, I chose to give a speech at a Peace Conference titled "Why I Chose I-W service." I rationalized I really chose I-W service but just didn't go any further and say that I had been rejected. My choosing not to be transparent added to my duplicity.

A month later, in July 1953, in order not to have to explain my classification to others, I went ahead and accepted a voluntary service assignment with MCC. This way, no one would suspect that I had been rejected.

After three weeks of orientation at the MCC headquarters, I was assigned to a reconstruction project in Topeka, Kansas, to help an African-American congregation rebuild their church after it was almost totally destroyed during the 1951 flood. This was not far from Marilyn's parents' home so I often hitch-hiked there for weekend visits when I could get away from my work.

MARILYN

On the surface, I accepted his explanation of why he was rejected by the military without further questioning, but deep in my heart, I asked myself: Why would they use the "too religious" excuse for someone who was a conscientious objector since that requires a deep Christian commitment? A lot of this was very puzzling to me, but I trusted that he was telling me the unvarnished truth. I suppose I was just blinded by love and dismissed it as irrelevant. I had some niggling suspicions, though, that he had been less than honest with me as well as others but had no way to prove it.

I graduated from nursing school in September 1953 and took my State Boards before I moved back to Kansas to work in the local hospital near my parents. Within a month I was notified that I had failed to pass two of my State Board exams—pediatrics and psychology. Carl visited me on weekends when he could get away from his work. Then at Thanksgiving, sitting at opposite ends of the sofa at my parents' home during one of our silences, Carl abruptly said in a matter-of-fact voice: "I guess maybe it's about time to announce our engagement." No fanfare, no getting down on his knees to pledge his love.

Why didn't I recognize the red flag called lack of enthusiasm? We had talked about marriage occasionally but, being the romantic I was, I still wanted him to actually ask me to marry him. I loved him and believed at some level he loved me, too. Being a proper, submissive woman, I did not question further.

Instead, I agreed it was time. I probably thought it was now or never. Later I wished I had asked, "What engagement?"

My parents were delighted when we told them the next morning. They respected Carl for his commitment to Christian ideals. We announced our engagement publicly at a dinner party with close friends. Instead of an engagement ring, which was forbidden in our religious circles, Carl gave me a gleaming silver tea set.

We set the date for our wedding and honeymoon to coincide with the April 10 date to re-take those two state board nursing exams. What a thing to do on our honeymoon! But that was the choice I had if I wanted to be a registered nurse. The next four months were blissful ones—a frenzied flurry of wedding preparations and two bridal showers. Mom, an accomplished seamstress, made my wedding dress and also the bridesmaids' and flower girl dresses.

As we anticipated our wedding, his letters became warmer and more emotionally expressive but also reflected some anxiety about it all. One of his letters dated January 14, 1954, read,

> *Marilyn, since we talked about getting married in March, I have been getting more and more eager for that day to come. If that plan doesn't work out it is going to be quite a let-down for me. I'm just like a child anticipating Christmas or something, nearly getting a jumping spell thinking about it. That doesn't sound quite like me, I know. Well, it's all because of the wonderful girl at the center of the anticipation.*
>
> *Still, I haven't forgotten the new responsibilities and obligations that the wedding will bring. Where will the money for the honeymoon come from? When will a young married couple ever get enough spare capital to pay back several years of schooling and several more to come, let alone furnish a home and provide for a baby when one comes! I've heard people say marriage has enough adjustments to make without financial burdens hanging over*

their heads. One thing I am confident of: there is a way through, but it is important to face things as they are.

Later that January, we were surprised when the MCC director asked us if we would consider a different voluntary service assignment after we were married. The agricultural migrant unit in the Central Valley of California in Fresno County needed a married couple to be unit leaders. Living in California sounded exciting. After praying about it and talking it over, we agreed to accept this assignment after we returned from our wedding trip. Carl completed his Voluntary Service assignment in Kansas the middle of March shortly before we were married.

Chapter 4

Early Disillusionment
March 1954–September 1959

MARILYN

It was cold and blustery on March 27, 1954, the day we were married—Marilyn Joyce Minter and J. Carl Wolgemuth. It was a simple but beautiful ceremony followed by a reception at the little country church where I grew up. Many family members, friends, and well-wishers celebrated with us at the reception. They sent us off with the traditional rice and confetti shower, wrote "Just Married" with soap on the car, smeared smelly cheese on the engine, and streamed toilet paper off the radio aerial. Tin cans rattled behind and a firecracker sizzled and popped when we started up the car. Finally we were launched on our long-awaited honeymoon to Pennsylvania, glad to be alone at last—Mr. and Mrs. Carl Wolgemuth. What magic lay in those words, I thought!

We headed east, meandered through the Ozark mountains, camped beside sparkling streams and arrived in Washington, D.C., on a warm April day with balmy breezes. It was perfect for strolling through the beautiful Japanese cherry trees during the annual Cherry Blossom Festival. Delicate pink blossoms at their peak encircled the Jefferson Memorial. The whole city was jammed with people. The Cherry Blossom Queen and the parade of cars from every state whizzed past us with the police car sirens blaring.

We arrived at Carl's parents' home in Pennsylvania where they had another reception for us. I took the State Board of

Nursing segments over again and didn't feel so embarrassed when seventeen of my classmates had to take the same two State Boards again too. Fortunately, I passed this time and later received my registered nurse license.

After saying goodbye to family, we traveled clear across the country to Fresno County, California. What new adventures would await us there?! For the next four years we were actively engaged in Christian service and church planting among the agricultural migrant families in the Central Valley along with other Voluntary Service members. We first lived in a small apartment with two single ladies. As newlyweds of just one month, it was tough to adjust to a group-living situation. At times, the stress and tension of the work and relationships were overwhelming.

During our first year of married life, I was disillusioned and puzzled about Carl's lack of enthusiasm and spontaneity in our sexual relationship. There was an absence of romantic affection that I attributed to newlywed jitters. I didn't want to be pushy. However, disturbing questions surfaced. Wasn't I attractive enough to him? What happened to that pre-marital excitement? I had expected eagerness. Instead, I had to initiate lovemaking. Sometimes he responded. Other times, he became nervous, anxious, withdrawn, and impotent.

I felt rejection, alienation, push-pull, approach-avoidance between us. We danced around issues. I over-functioned, and he under-functioned. Communication was a chore; much like a hide-and-seek game. Power struggles became common—pushivity vs. passivity. When I pushed for an explanation of his distancing, he passively isolated and gave me the silent treatment.

His moods were increasingly morose and ambivalent about an intimate relationship. He became terribly anxious whenever I wanted to give and receive affection. He perspired profusely until the bed sheet was soaked. He didn't want to cuddle up close or be touched when we slept together. He made some excuse about having slept alone all his life and not being able to adjust to sleeping with another person. I often cried myself to sleep, not knowing what to do.

He became moody, irritable, and withdrawn, barely speaking to me for long periods. I must be unlovable. What was wrong with me? This wasn't the way marriage was supposed to be, was it? I tried hard to please him, ease his anxiety, and not demand anything of him.

After two years, I knew something was dreadfully abnormal. Finally, I mustered the courage to come right out and ask him what was going on with him. It was then that he admitted he was not sexually attracted to women but instead fantasized about having sex with young males between ages twelve to twenty-five. He talked about when he was fifteen and infatuated with "Bobby," a thirteen-year-old neighbor boy. He said he still looked for a "Bobby-type" person to love. He made it clear that I wasn't his "type." For him, an attractive female would be the "Twiggy" type: tall, lithe, slender, small breasts, narrow hips, and about fifteen—the antithesis of what I was: short, a bit overweight, curvaceous. So why did he marry me? What motivated him to get married at all?

All this was a huge blow to my self-esteem. For the first time, I was strongly tempted to seek help from a counselor but had no clue where to look for one. I was riddled with guilt and embarrassment at the thought of sharing these problems with a stranger. After all, we were in Christian service. Since there was no one I could confide in, my secret was buried deeper and deeper. Nothing in my sheltered life experience prepared me for being married to a gay man. In that era, the term *gay* was tossed around blithely to mean "fun."

Homosexuality was referred to as a sin in the Scriptures. Preachers wouldn't touch the subject of sexual orientation except in passing. I was exposed to the concept in college psychology class and in nursing school, but I dismissed it as irrelevant at that time.

Not fully understanding what all this meant, I continued to blame myself for his discontent and disinterest, quite sure I wasn't what he wanted in a wife. I did all I knew how to do to be a good wife. However, that concept was becoming more elusive to me all the time. What did it mean to be a good wife in this situation? He was less and less responsive to my attempts to attract him with my femininity. Even books and magazine articles about "Can this marriage be saved?" didn't address the problems we were dealing with. Somehow I managed to muddle through and put on a happy face to the public.

Another contentious issue grew between us. Being on a church-related assignment, Carl, who wanted to be theologically correct, asked me to let my hair grow and cover it up under a prayer covering again. Inside I rebelled, though outwardly I complied since my aim was to be the obedient wife and to please this man. If only I could be the perfect wife, then maybe he would like me better.

Three years into our marriage, we were ecstatic when I became pregnant with our first daughter. I carried Joyce Elaine full term but, sadly, she was stillborn. She's buried in a tiny grave near Fresno. My world was shattered. I ached for support from Carl, but he had no idea how to be supportive to another person. So we each grieved alone, unable to share our deepest feelings with each other. We went on with our lives in a superficial way but inside, the ache was unbearable.

Despite our grief, we went ahead with plans for Spanish language study so we could enhance our ministry to the Spanish-speaking migrants. We moved to our church college in southern California, near Los Angeles, where we had many friends and acquaintances. Three days a week a Spanish speaking person tutored us in conversational Spanish, using the textbook from Mexico City College in Mexico.

For financial reasons, we took three jobs offered to us: we managed the college snack bar, I was college nurse, and Carl was dorm supervisor for twelve male students. It never occurred to me that, given his sexual orientation, it was a bad idea for him to supervise college men. I see now that I was naive as well as in huge denial. I assumed this was where we were supposed to be, so we settled into a small apartment in the college men's dorm.

Before too many weeks had elapsed, I was faced with another awesome dilemma when Carl revealed to me that several times after dark he stripped naked and walked outside back of the apartment. He denied that anyone saw him, but who knows? I knew exhibitionism was a serious offense if he was caught. I began to understand why he had little or no interest in intimacy—he was focused on himself. This was too big and heavy for me! I felt desperate. I had to do something. But what? Intense anxiety plagued me. I secretly called a friend for the name of a Christian counselor and I made an appointment. Carl was not at all pleased that I had done this, but he reluctantly agreed to go along.

Dr. Eiler was a typical, bearded psychologist, congenial but formidable to us first-timers. We went to our first appointment with great trepidation since we had never dared go to a counselor. The rigid attitudes and subtle messages given by our church leaders rang loudly in our ears—missionaries and people in Christian service aren't supposed to admit they struggle with emotional issues! Maybe you're not spiritual enough. Just pray harder and everything will turn out all right. It's not okay to let other people know you have problems. Have faith and trust God for victory over them.

Even with all that religiosity and emotional static bouncing around in our heads, we attended group therapy for several weeks and listened to others talk freely about their personal problems. But it was almost impossible for either of us to open up. A lot of shame was connected with why we were there. It was much too scary to be honest. If Carl couldn't disclose his secrets, it was futile to keep going.

That school year I stumbled along the best I could, struggled with grief over the loss of our first-born, kept up a smiley face. Yet, I was desperate and hurting inside for lack of intimacy and emotional support. My sporadic attempts at sharing my feelings with Carl only produced his contempt and silence. Instead, clueless, closed, and distant, he kept tightly held feelings and secrets within himself.

That fall and spring we attended a small Spanish-speaking Nazarene church where we practiced what we were learning in our tutored classes. Several evenings a week Carl taught English as a Second Language to braceros, men from Mexico on special work permits, who lived in nearby camps. This gave him more opportunities to learn to speak Spanish.

When the school year ended in May 1959 we drove many long miles to Mexico City to continue the advanced course of Spanish study at Mexico City College for eight weeks. One of the men in Carl's English class who was returning to Mexico had invited us to live with him and his family in Mexico City, and we gratefully accepted his offer. Humberto, his wife Concha and their young daughters, Aida and Bette, lived in a modest home. They spoke only Spanish, so it was total immersion in elementary conversational Spanish—the best way to learn another language. We enjoyed the family setting and Concha's excellent Mexican cooking.

I suffered severe headaches almost every day due to stress from the intense language learning, high altitude, strange culture, and our strained relationship. We had some fun in between, though: sightseeing, deep-sea fishing, browsing the colorful Indian markets, visiting the Wycliffe Bible Translators headquarters on Sunday evenings, and hearing the missionaries tell about their work.

As the summer progressed, the alienation between us became unbearable. I needed some relief from the stress and emotional pain accumulated over these five years of married life. Somehow, after four weeks, I mustered the courage to book a flight to Wichita, Kansas and take a bus to my parents' home. They were not thrilled to see me because they strongly opposed my decision to leave Carl. Consequently, the time with them proved to be less than satisfactory. When I tried to explain my reasons, they couldn't comprehend anything I was trying to say. Instead they laid more guilt trips on me! The not-so-subtle message came through: a faithful wife stays true to her vows; you stay with your spouse no matter what. No support there!

I worked part-time at the local hospital while I pondered my situation. I felt guilty for leaving and yet enjoyed this strange new freedom. Did I want to stay married to a man who manipulated me with his contempt and silent moods? What were my options? He projected the unassailable image of being such a devoted Christian, committed to mission work, and had all the right religious vocabulary. It must be me who was wrong.

So many thoughts raced through my head. For the first time, I seriously contemplated divorce. In our circle of friends divorce was unthinkable, unacceptable. If I divorced Carl, I would surely be blamed and forever labeled a bad wife. I wasn't ready to be ostracized. A little voice said: *Just suck up the pain and pretend there is no problem.* I had no one I could talk to so I coped the best I could. I smiled a lot. I had no idea yet how to express feelings, what assertiveness meant, or how to take care of myself. The Bible says to deny ourselves, think of others before we think of ourselves. That had been drilled into me in countless ways through the years!

After Carl finished the Spanish course, he was to help with the Mexico Youth For Christ evangelistic campaign in Merida, Yucatan, for two weeks. While he was there, I received a letter from him inviting me to come to Merida for his last week. The letter also included a surprise—a plane ticket. He sounded so sincere. Cautiously I considered this option, puzzled about what I should do. Did he really want me back, or was I just a convenience to him? What did he want out of this relationship? Now I know that I trusted him too quickly and was too easily persuaded. But I truly wanted to do my part to make our marriage work. Years later, I learned that is part of co-dependency.

Finally, with mixed feelings—guilty for even considering a permanent separation and feeling obliged to stay with him—I wrapped up things at home and at my work then took off for Merida. Those marriage vows I had made—"for better or for worse, in sickness or in health, for richer or poorer"—were ringing in my ears.

CARL

I did have some romantic notions and fleeting feelings of affection, and the thought of having sex excited me. But, I wasn't deeply in love with her. I wanted companionship with someone like-minded, someone who loved me, and I knew that Marilyn loved me. At some level, I wanted someone to take care of me. Marilyn was a nurse and would be a good person to do that. In my mind, these things added up to reasons enough to marry. After all, it was the normal and socially acceptable thing to do at my age. I didn't want to appear different.

About this time in my life I was ready to drop conservative conformity regardless of what gossip resulted. One of the things in my life that changed was the plain clerical-collared coat I usually wore. For the first time, I bought a blue suit with a double-breasted coat and chose a blue-and-white tie with diagonal stripes. This turned out to be the suit and tie I wore at our wedding.

Wearing a tie was a revolutionary, emotional issue for me. I no longer believed that wearing a plain suit without a tie was a statement of faith and measure of spirituality. I felt a large dose of excitement to be released from the repressive constraints of dressing a certain way just to please authority figures. Also, since a ring ceremony was forbidden, we waited to put on the rings we bought for each other until after we left on our honeymoon. This was deceptive, I must admit.

After we were married, I chose to not write letters to my parents. Those were the days of carbon-copies, and since Marilyn was a prolific letter writer, I figured she could write carbon copies to send to all our families. Twenty years later, it dawned on her that by doing that she was taking that responsibility away from me. With that realization, she "resigned" as go-between and left it up to me to decide if I wanted to write to my parents. It was more than a year before I could do that. I'm sure my parents were hurt that I chose to distance myself.

The first time I disclosed my homosexual side to Marilyn was when she confronted me after I couldn't make love over a period of time. It was then I finally told her the real reason for my 4-F draft classification. She couldn't quite take it all in.

In 1959, after Marilyn flew from Mexico City back to Kansas, I completed the eight-week course of Spanish study at Mexico City College after which I worked with the Mexico Youth For Christ evangelization campaign. I held revival-type meetings in Spanish in Merida, Yucatan, for two weeks. It was a good opportunity to use my newly acquired conversational Spanish as I worked alongside several young male students at the Bible school there. That brought a whole new set of temptations for me to sexually fantasize.

I did miss Marilyn, though, after she went back to Kansas, so I sent her a letter that included a plane ticket along with an emotional plea for her to re-join me for the remainder of my time in Merida. After she arrived, the friendly Yucatecan families hosted us for a week. We each slept in a hand-woven Yucatan string hammock. We adapted quite well to dirt floors, thatched roofs, different foods, customs, dress, the hot and humid climate, and the melodic Mayan language.

After leaving Merida, we went by train to the neighboring state of Chiapas, Mexico, to the headquarters of Missionary Aviation Fellowship. We had arranged to fly over the vast green jungle in a Cessna MAF plane to a remote and primitive part of the country to visit one of the Bible Translation outposts. It was thrilling to see missionaries in action. The language work fascinated me and the challenge of translating the New Testament for a Bible-less people-group captivated my imagination. We both had been feeling that this was what God was calling us to do with our lives. This experience clinched our decision to work toward that goal.

Chapter 5

The Five Year Mark
September 1959–July 1965

MARILYN

By the end of the summer course of study in Mexico, our heads and hearts were reeling with questions and uncertainties as we headed back to Los Angeles pondering what our next step would be. How would God lead us from this point on?

I was intrigued by the unique medical challenges the missionary nurses faced among the tribal people. I knew that my three years of nursing school would be totally inadequate for this type of ministry and I would need further training. The Bible Institute of Los Angeles (BIOLA) was well known for courses in public health, tropical medicine, dentistry, and laboratory procedures, but to live in sprawling Los Angeles was a formidable prospect since we had always lived in either rural or small-town settings!

So many decisions to make—where in this huge city would we begin looking for a place to live? What jobs could we get that would pay the bills?

In our search for a place to live, we found the cutest little two-bedroom house tucked away at the bottom of a cliff next to a city park in the Highland Park area of Los Angeles. The friendly landlord and his wife, with their heavy Austrian accent, lived next door and rented it furnished for $85 a month. Lemon, orange, and avocado trees graced the front and back yards. It was an idyllic location, typical southern California.

The freeway and public transportation were close by for easy access to school, work, and shopping. Moneywise we had exhausted nearly all our savings with study and travel so it was touch-and-go for us to make ends meet. That was a minor glitch, though, compared to the major glitches in our relationship.

By then, we had been married more than five years. The emotional distance between us was greater than ever. Oh, we were friendly and polite enough to each other—most of the time—like ships passing in the night on the high seas. My heart became so heavy due to his rejection of me as a sexual partner that I moved to another bedroom. I needed to distance myself from this person who was so emotionally unavailable. This was the first place we ever lived that I had the luxury of my own bedroom. It had its advantages, but I felt isolated and lonely. As usual, we both did a good job of keeping the "ideal couple" image intact by pretending everything was A-OK.

An added stress was emergency surgery I needed for a ruptured ovarian cyst that left me wondering if I could ever get pregnant again. The doctor was optimistic, but the prospects seemed quite remote due to our infrequent times of marital intimacy.

We located another Christian counselor and had a few sessions with him, but Carl could not, or would not, disclose his core issues: his indifference toward marital intimacy, his same-sex attractions, his penchant for exhibitionism. His ambivalence prevented him from sharing his thoughts and feelings—he often refused to talk in a session. It soon became evident this was not going anywhere, so it was back to square one. Counseling was doomed to become an exercise in futility. It was like trying to pry open a door that was securely bolted shut.

First semester I worked as an obstetrical nurse at the Salvation Army's Booth Memorial Hospital for Unmarried Mothers. This was a unique opportunity to help mostly teenage girls who were at a major crossroads in their lives and making important life decisions. Delivering their babies was my primary work, but often I took time to coach them in their academic work since the school rooms were in the hospital. Second semester I attended classes at BIOLA in mid-town Los Angeles to better prepare myself for medical work in primitive areas and graduated in May 1960.

While living in LA, Carl worked at several jobs and I was busy between being an Avon saleslady, keeping up with classes, and delivering babies part-time. As we sought God's direction for our lives we held open the option of returning to the work among the migrant people. In communication with our friends still in the MCC work back in Central California, they told us the situation for agricultural migrants was changing rapidly— the migrant camps were being closed by health department decree and the work the team had been doing was coming to an end so it was not feasible for us to even consider returning there.

A still, small voice kept nudging us toward Bible translation work somewhere in Latin America. In spring of 1960, our next step of faith was to register for the required summer linguistic courses given by Wycliffe Bible Translators at the University of Oklahoma with classes to begin in June. To get the necessary funds for that, we sold many of our earthly possessions before heading to Norman, Oklahoma.

Student living quarters were in the ancient, dingy, unadorned army barracks furnished with bunk beds, group bathrooms, and NO air conditioning! The Wycliffe faculty and more than 100 students, who were prospective missionary translators, lived in these dreary buildings. The studies were intensive and we sweated it out in the hot, humid Oklahoma climate.

Since we were in an academic environment, with young, attractive males all around us, I braced myself again for trouble in our relationship. For whatever reason, this time Carl was more attentive and intimate. By mid-summer we were pleasantly sur-

prised to discover that we were pregnant—even with the op-
pressive heat and bunk beds working against us. Good news in-
deed! I was anxious over the painful memory of losing our first
baby. How hopeful should I allow myself to be? I didn't relish
the disappointment of losing another baby.

During the next fall and winter we lived with Carl's parents
in Pennsylvania. I did some part-time nursing and Carl worked
at a print shop. The pregnancy was uneventful this time, and
our healthy baby girl, Carolyn Joy, was born on March 6, 1961.
Caring for a baby seemed to take more and more time so we
coasted along the best we could.

Would this bring us together and make a difference in our
relationship? It didn't. Carl was referred to a Christian psychiatrist with whom he continued sessions for several months. It
seemed like no amount of professional help could penetrate
Carl's shell of denial and resistance to "fess up" to what the issues were that troubled him. Moving from place to place,
changing counselors as we were doing, may have been factors in
the lack of solutions to problems that had developed over many
years.

The next summer we attended the advanced linguistic
courses at University of Oklahoma. Another blistering, sticky
three months was in store for us. I don't know how we made it
through because the humidity and heat exhausted us! This time
around, the studies were even more concentrated than the summer before! Trying to study in the intense heat with a three-
month-old baby was a brand new experience!

Our finances were very tight, and we barely had enough
money for milk and baby food. We experienced the Lord's
faithfulness when we were down to almost nothing. It was then
that we would find an anonymous money gift in our mailbox.
Later we discovered that faculty and staff were God's angels.
This was our introduction to this new experience called living
by faith. It was scary, I must admit, to realize we were totally dependent on God to provide through other people.

By the end of the summer we had applied for membership in Wycliffe. After what seemed like endless, required paper work, we were accepted as new members!! WOW! Where would this step of faith take us?? Classes were over and we literally had no money—just enough to get us to my parents' home in Kansas. They graciously invited us to live with them while we prepared for the next big step in our journey. All new Wycliffe members were required to go through three months of orientation to primitive living conditions at the Jungle Training Camp located in southern Mexico.

We were scheduled for the first session beginning in November 1961, but our plans were interrupted and our trip delayed when I needed emergency surgery again. While I recuperated, my parents provided loving care for eight-month-old Carolyn. Carl worked for my uncle as a carpenter to earn the funds we were required to have in hand before going to Mexico. People in my home church were so supportive to us and gave generously toward my medical and hospital expenses.

This was an exceptionally stressful time, not knowing when or if our plans would work out. Our relationship was tolerable although still not satisfactory—sexual union was an on-off thing, more off than on, depending on Carl's moods. We still promoted the "ideal couple" image, though, by singing duets together. I must admit that we sang quite well together and were often asked to sing when we spoke in churches about our work with the mission.

By February 1962, my recovery had gone well enough for the three of us to travel by train to Mexico. The primitive jungle training was exhausting for everyone but became even more so for me. With a child to care for and having had recent surgery, I felt the need for emotional support more than ever—if only Carl knew how to be emotionally available! He loved the outdoors life and took pride in his skills for improvising with limited resources. Outwardly, he was calm, composed, competent, showing very little emotion. No one would ever guess the inner struggles that plagued us.

Tropical living conditions were physically strenuous for me. I felt tired much of the time, alone, unloved, and cried myself to sleep nearly every night. Carolyn must have felt the ever-present tension, too. She was adaptable, though, to the many changes involved in this different life-style, which included sleeping in a jungle hammock, eating tortillas, wearing diapers dried over an open fire because of the high humidity, learning to walk on the uneven terrain.

After the training course was over, we were invited to continue on as staff members for the next year helping to train the next wave of new members. One-year-old Carolyn kept me busy. She had learned to walk by this time and required careful supervision to prevent her from wandering off into dangerous places. Even at that early age she was fascinated by horses. One time I rescued her from underneath the belly of Smoky, the gentle horse! There was little time or emotional energy to improve our communication. When someone commented on what a happy family we were, I wanted to yell and scream back, If you only knew! But I just smiled sweetly and said, "Thank you." And so I plodded on, never contemplating an alternative. We had set our sights on our goals and fully intended to reach them.

CARL

During our year in Los Angeles I obtained my commercial driver's license and drove school buses for the Pasadena district and also the Allen Charter Bus company. I tried my hand at selling Fuller Brushes, Bible encyclopedias, and sets of Christian music records. It didn't take me long to decide sales work was not for me.

After two summers of linguistic study and being trained for primitive jungle living, we continued to feel a strong urge toward doing Bible translation work somewhere in the world, preferably in Latin America since we had studied Spanish.

Three people-groups in Mexico with unwritten languages needed a translation team. We chose the Aztec people-group in southern Veracruz who speak the Isthmus Nahuatl language.

In preparation for that assignment, we went through a process called deputation—speaking in churches, challenging people to earnestly pray for the work of Bible translation. The Lord graciously provided us with prayer and financial partners as we drove from Pennsylvania to California.

We fully intended to return to Mexico to live and work with the Aztec people but another surprising turn of events came while we were at Wycliffe's headquarters California. We were asked to consider a temporary assignment as personnel managers at the Pavilion of 2000 Tribes that was in the process of being built for the 1964-1965 World's Fair to be held in New York City.

Was this God's direction for us at this time? Given our persistent personal problems, were we even spiritually and emotionally ready to do language learning and translation work? After giving it a lot of thought and diligently seeking God's will, we consented to take up this assignment. It meant driving all the way back over the route we had just taken and telling many of the same people about the change in our plans. Everyone else was surprised, too!

Thus, in January 1964, we wended our way to the Big Apple, like Abraham in the Bible, going to an unknown country, without a clue as to what awaited us. We arrived in the Big City on a cold, windy day right after a huge snow storm. Snow was piled six feet high from where the snow plow had tried to clear the streets. We had the name and address of the Hepzibah House, a missionary hostel in downtown New York City, where temporary housing had been arranged for us. A big, drafty old house in Flushing was being remodeled where we were to live along with other Wycliffe members assigned to the Fair.

Amid all our apparent success with our ministry in missions, I continued to be plagued by deviant thinking and lack of desire for intimacy so, this time, I took the initiative to locate a Christian counselor. During the eighteen months we lived in New York I wish I could say that the counseling made a big difference. Maybe "JBND"—a just-barely noticeable-difference. Temporarily, I was keenly aware that I had a long, l-o-n-g way to go before I could overcome the dysfunctional way that I viewed the complicated issues around my sexual orientation as they related to working together in a marriage.

From January 1964 to July 1965, we were both heavily involved in a variety of activities: I was housing coordinator for our Wycliffe colleagues who came for six-week rotations to serve on staff at the pavilion. Marilyn was in charge of cooking meals for the group which at times numbered thirty people! The fair closed for the winter and we continued living in the Flushing house. This gave us more time to focus on where we were in our relationship.

MARILYN

Carl resisted sharing with me what he was working on in his counseling sessions. Since the outcome would affect me also, it was hard for me not to ask him questions. I'm sure I bugged him much too often. His secretiveness and indifference sure bugged me! He let me know in no uncertain terms that he needed "privacy." We had many discussions about keeping secrets in a relationship. Secrets versus privacy—he didn't seem to think there was anything wrong with either one. "Everybody needs privacy" he would tell me. This attitude must stem from resentment of his parents' intrusion into his life during his growing-up years. Sometimes, actually, we related more as parent-child than husband-wife. We certainly weren't able to work well together as a team.

The World's Fair opened again in April, and we stayed until we completed our time there in July 1965. Now maybe we could get on with our goals for learning the Aztec language and begin Bible translation.

Chapter 6

Going to Mexico
July 1965–July 1974

MARILYN

When our assignment in New York City was over, we were finally ready to head south for Mexico that we had been planning for so long—to begin language learning, linguistic analysis and eventually Scripture translation. On arrival in Mexico City, we bought supplies and took care of government paperwork before going on to our tribal location 500 miles further south.

I was not aware to what extent Carl was plagued with anxiety since he seldom shared his deeper self with me. In our naiveté, we plodded on and continued with our plans as if all our personal problems would evaporate by themselves. It was like we were on a space ship trajectory with nothing to stop us unless something drastic would happen. How could we know that eventually something disastrous would happen, and it would become unbearably stressful, even to the breaking point? Despite all the struggles and hurdles facing us, I personally trusted God to guide us and care for us.

Being a perfectionist, Carl brooded over any little thing that unsettled him. Triggers for his anxiety usually included ambivalence and doubts. These always spelled trouble in our relationship. It was very hard for him to identify his feelings and share his thoughts with me. Weren't we in this together? Were we both convinced this was what God wanted us to do? Surely God would not call just one of us. It was hard for me to accept his doubts. I had committed myself to this task. I cared about the impoverished Aztec people who didn't have any written Scriptures in the language of their hearts.

In addition to all the daunting adjustments of living in a primitive environment, we were trying to cope with a dysfunctional relationship. Could he actually follow through? We were at a point of no return—like a marriage ceremony, no turning back. It would have been humiliating to tell our support people that we got cold feet at the last minute! What would they think? Me, the people-pleaser. All I knew how to do at this point was to shove doubts and fears into the dark closet of denial and continue with plans for our new life.

In September 1965 we settled in to our new surroundings in Mecayapan, Veracruz, Mexico. This remote setting in the tropics required major living adjustments. Even in our previous jungle training we had never been this isolated before. There was one single-lane rutted road for trucks to deliver beer—but only in dry weather. The only way for us to relax, replenish our supplies, and get mail once a month was to hike five miles through the jungle. We had to hike over narrow, rough walking trails through two rushing rivers to where our car was parked and then drive fifty miles on paved road to the market town.

The house we lived in was like most of the houses in that area except ours had a corrugated metal roof instead of thatch. The mud walls, dirt floor, and lots of varmints were what we had to contend with. There was no phone service, electricity, refrigeration, or indoor plumbing.

This rustic, rural living environment was destined to shed a harsh light on the glaring weaknesses in our relationship. We were the only English speakers for many miles around. Until we learned to speak the Aztec language, the three of us were forced to rely on each other for emotional support. Each of us inwardly battled the complicated issues we had brought with us.

But there was plenty of work to keep me from dwelling on personal problems—language and culture assimilation, visiting families in their thatched-roof huts, providing medical and dental assistance, being on call 24/7, and home-schooling Carolyn for eight years. It was after family bedtime stories and devotions with Carolyn that I felt the acute need for closeness with someone with whom I could share in depth. I yearned for affection, emotional support, empathy, and understanding.

The efforts I put forth to encourage and support Carl didn't go both ways. My idea of marriage was that both partners were to share equally in the give and take of a relationship. But in our case, I gave and he took. I hadn't yet learned how to stop enabling another person's dysfunction or how to be more assertive. Carl's changeable moods were a big factor in his insensitive approach to intimacy. I felt trapped and isolated in a lifeless marriage. Our attempts to have family devotions became an on-off endeavor, as well. Sometimes God seemed far away. Doing His work must count for something, I told myself. I could only trust that He would use our efforts to further his kingdom despite floundering in this situation.

After five years of diligently learning the language and staying focused on our goals, we were due for a year's furlough in the States. I was more than ready for a break from being on call twenty-four hours a day. Carl affirmed me in my desire to go back to our alma mater to earn my bachelor's of science degree in nursing. We headed to Pennsylvania where I buried myself in my studies and graduated in May 1971. Going back to college at age 40 as a non-traditional student was enjoyable and exhilarating.

By spring of 1973, the tension between us had increased exponentially. My faith in God's guidance was definitely a steadying influence that got me through these last few years. Both of us were heavily involved in the translation work and I continued to minister through medical work. Our command of the language at this point impressed the Aztec people. They loved us, brought us gifts of food, invited us to their fiestas, weddings, funerals. We worked alongside them in community projects, such as laying pipes for a clean water system. A small but growing nucleus of Christians was willing to help us in the translation work. For me there was definitely a sense of satisfaction in living among our Aztec friends that compensated for our faltering marriage.

A major stress factor was when Susie, our native friend and language helper, died suddenly of a cerebral hemorrhage. Her husband Gene and one-year old David were left to mourn her passing. After her death, Gene continued to help us on the language and we offered to care for little David, an adorable toddler just learning to walk. It was so different having a child to care for again.

I often wondered why things happened the way they did, but I was confident that He takes us through these times for reasons only He knows. He makes no mistakes.

CARL

The challenge of tribal living looked like we were about to climb Mount Everest. The following journal notes, written after we arrived in Mexico, speak loudly about the doubts and ambivalence I was having with a long-term commitment of language study and translation work.

August 5, 1965

Would it be feasible to think of giving village life a try on a tentative basis? Fifty percent of my motivation to do this would be to satisfy friends and supporters who know that we have been talking about the Isthmus Aztecs for at least three years. The other fifty percent would be to satisfy my own dream of purposeful work.

September 6, 1965

In yesterday morning's message at the English-speaking church in Mexico City the young minister spoke about the necessity of faith. As he talked, I was convicted of the large amount of unbelief in my approach to the Word and prayer. Without faith it is impossible to please God. I easily absorb the spirit of doubt. I confessed this to God and asked Him to give me faith to replace the unfaith. "Anyone who wants to come to God must believe that there is a God and that He will reveal Himself to those who sincerely look for Him" (Heb. 11:6b).

A small adobe hut with a metal roof was our home in the remote Aztec village of Mecayapan, population 5,000. The community was nestled in the tropical jungles of southern Veracruz, Mexico. We were surrounded by friendly neighbors. Four-year old Carolyn was challenged with learning another culture and two more languages—Spanish and Isthmus Nahuatl.

Our primary tasks were to learn to speak and do linguistic analysis on Nahuatl, the official name of the language spoken by the Aztec people. There were no written materials in the language because it was still only a spoken language. So we could only learn to speak Nahuatl by listening to conversations, recording them and applying the techniques we had learned in those heavy-duty linguistic courses. First we analyzed the sounds and grammar of this language and then chose appropriate symbols for an alphabet based on the Spanish letters.

As we gained fluency in the language, we became friends with the native people, held reading classes, attended the nightly church services, translated New Testament Scriptures, and helped with community projects. I spent most days and evenings with the men in the village consulting with officials and working on the Scripture translation goals with native speakers.

All the while, I felt growing frustration with my work and with my marriage due to my sexual ambivalence and the anxiety it caused. Sporadically, we considered being honest with our director in Mexico City about the personal difficulties we were having. We couldn't even talk about it between ourselves, much less with someone in authority over us. My May 22 journal entry reflected this frustration.

May 22, 1970

> I am too often irritated by people. This morning I realized the irritation is due to the demands of the people on my time for things that to me are secondary. There is so little interest in the materials I am translating, which is the main reason I'm here, and which I want them to want. Now the thought has come to me that these very demands give me an opportunity to cheerfully serve the people's needs and do what I can to interest people, if only I will realize it at the time. But if I let my irritation prevail, that very attitude will repel people from becoming interested.

> After Marilyn graduated in June 1971 with her BSN degree, the end of our furlough was fast approaching and it was time for us to go back to Mexico. Recurring serious doubts about returning to the life and work weighed heavily on my heart. I couldn't talk about my struggle so I kept it inside. Out of a sense of obligation, not love of the people or the work, I decided it was important to continue what I had started. So in July we returned to Mecayapan, our village home.

February 1972

> I finally admitted to myself that I intensely dislike translation work. I glanced at my book "Notes on Translation" today and realized that I hate the very discussion of the subject. I believe this feeling of depression I have is associated with the fact that I don't have the self-discipline to do all the desk work that should be done by a linguist. I'm no linguist. And pretending to be one is demoralizing. I can't under-

stand why God should have brought us here to something that isn't even down my line.

Procrastination has been one of my major problems for a long time. I never learned how to set specific goals for myself. I easily became overwhelmed with the immensity and the complexity of the language program. Making monthly reports to our project supervisor became increasingly irksome for me. I felt the need for additional personnel to share the load but knew that there was little hope of that happening since there were more people groups needing personnel than there were people to fill them.

March 1972

Even our marital happiness depends on faith. The last few months I have been living on an entirely non-spiritual plane without exercising any sort of daily faith and discipline. I have grown steadily away from Marilyn. Last night we aired this again, but only after Marilyn had an emotional outburst after returning from a week in the city. We agreed to pray for each other specifically. I confessed my need for getting rid of bitterness and pride and other wrong attitudes. Already this morning I can feel some affection. I dreamed that we prayed for a miracle.

After Susie died, Gene's grief was extra hard on me. I spent so much emotional energy listening to him talk out his heart and release his pent-up emotions. I realized these intimate times posed a real dilemma for me—sexual attraction. Finally, we mustered the courage to confide in our director about our marital struggles and the deep doubts I was having. His advice was that we take advantage of the mission's counseling department in southern California and also take some time to rest and revitalize our spirits.

We were offered an ideal living situation in Fountain Valley, California—a house-sitting opportunity by one of our former Wycliffe members who was away for the summer. Twice a week for two months we counseled with Dr. W in his office. This proved helpful in sorting out some of the personal problems and recent traumatic experiences we encountered.

During our sessions with Dr. W., I discovered a lot about the uneven parenting I received. In his opinion, I had been emotionally abused and severely stunted in my ability to relate to other people, especially a woman in a marriage relationship. He believed that my emotional development was arrested by age fifteen. That made sense to me, coinciding with my infatuation with Bobbie, the neighbor boy. Dr. W. challenged me to be honest with Marilyn and tell her what irritated me. That was a big order because, in my inner child's mind, she was a parental figure and I wanted to avoid upsetting her.

MARILYN

I don't know what more I expected Carl to come up with in counseling. He had already told me he wasn't in love with me when we married. He made it clear, again, that I wasn't his type. What he came up was this: "I feel very irritated when I step barefooted on the water that you drip on the bathmat after you get out of the shower." I knew he was a perfectionist, but this blew me away. This type of honesty was out of character for him. I'm sure it took a lot of courage for him to be straight with me.

You can be sure that from then on I was careful to put an extra towel down first before I got out of the tub or shower. If I could avoid irritating him by making simple changes, I was more than willing to do it. Twenty five years later he related more examples of things that irritated him—things I couldn't change—that proved to be much more problematic.

The summer ended with our issues still unresolved. We knew we would need more counseling eventually. We chose to return to Mexico since we had left some major projects unfinished. This time in the village we experienced some positive sides of our work: the Aztec people were learning to read the Scriptures in their language and using them in their church services.

We spent the next year in our village home, but the tension and emotional distance between us were as heavy as ever. Carl and I had an ongoing disagreement about discipline and guidance of our daughter, now thirteen. He had a very laid-back attitude and rarely gave her guidance. For example, he allowed her to ride our horse anywhere she wanted to, including away from the village on jungle trails by herself. Much to my dismay, Carl never wanted to set any limits with her about how far, how long, or where she could ride. His reasoning: He had been so restricted and repressed growing up that he had vowed he would not put restrictions on his child.

I uneasily observed the interest the village teenage boys had in her. At age thirteen, she was of marriageable age according to the village customs. Carl had his usual, indifferent attitude about it. He may have even welcomed that option. I don't know. He wouldn't talk about it with me. Whiffs of gossip told me that some of the local boys were interested in having her as a wife since she knew how to speak the language, grind corn, make tortillas, wash clothes on the rocks in the river, and other things that a good village wife would do.

I had other concerns about this issue also. First, it went against the local culture for a young girl to be riding a horse; second, the people couldn't understand why she was allowed to ride alone. I wondered what message that sent to our friends in the villages. Many times I had expressed to Carl my fear of her being attacked, kidnapped, or molested out on the trails. Each time I brought it up, he ignored my apprehension. I felt the whole issue was out of my control. One day, in spring 1974, she rode off to who knows where and was gone for a couple of hours. I couldn't take it any longer. As we stood there in our little kitchen, I told him again, in no uncertain terms, what my fears were. I'll never forget his telling me that he actually worried about his own ability to control himself with her.

I was stunned. This was the tipping point. My maternal instinct kicked in big time. I thought to myself, *I've got to protect my daughter! If I don't, no one else will.* I said, "This is the last straw. I'm leaving this place and taking Carolyn with me. You can just stay here for all I care." I was enraged and intended to protect my daughter at all cost, like a mother bear guarding her cub.

All of a sudden the bottom had dropped out of everything familiar. For awhile I was very depressed, but determined to get out of this situation. Finally, after all these years, it dawned on me that he had no protective fatherly feelings for her and was totally oblivious to the danger signals. He was more of a big brother than a father, living vicariously through her, not restricting her like he had been restricted.

Carolyn was adamant about wanting to stay where she could ride her horse. I tried to explain to her why it was best for us to leave: We needed to get some more counseling so we could hopefully stay together as a family; since she would be in eighth grade, it was time that she be with English-speaking peers. This was as much as I thought she could understand. I did not tell her the whole reason.

With a heavy heart around these increasingly troublesome personal problems, I prepared to leave this man. Not an easy decision. But I was resolute and persistent. I could see no other way out. I didn't have a firm plan in mind but knew I had to get out of there—and fast. Carolyn and I would hike over the trail to catch a second-class bus to go to Mexico City and from there decide what to do. I really didn't care if Carl went with us or not, but he couldn't bear the thought of staying behind. He insisted on going with us. So we closed up the house and went to Mexico City. Our director there sensed my frustration and despair and urged us to resume counseling with Dr. W., who by then had moved his office to the International Linguistic Center in Dallas, the major training center for new Wycliffe personnel.

It wasn't easy for me leave the work we had come to do and say goodbye to my dear Aztec friends—the people I had grown to love. My depression was so deep I didn't know how I would tolerate driving with him those 1,700 miles to Dallas.

Chapter 7

Pulling Up Stakes—Twice
July 1974–December 1982

MARILYN

It was with apprehension and heavy hearts that Carl, Carolyn, and I settled into a modest rented house. Counseling sessions got underway immediately. Carl was usually morose, moody, and uncommunicative. We slept in separate bedrooms. I worked part time as a volunteer receptionist at the Center for the first semester. Carl worked on assignments that Dr. W gave him. After some initial reverse culture shock, it didn't take us long to adjust, since we had Wycliffe friends who also lived in the area.

Our prayer and financial supporters wanted to know: "When are you going back to Mexico?" We wrote:

> *"We can only say that we have no plans to go back permanently at this time. After earnestly seeking the Lord's direction, we requested an assignment here in the States for the next few years. The counseling program we've started is meeting a real need for us. Carl needs the kind of structured work environment provided by his present responsibilities in Printing Arts Department. He's found a great deal of satisfaction the last six months supervising the computerized typesetting operations and helping other translators get their New Testaments ready for printing. Carolyn is in eighth grade and needs a stable environment, too. We all need a settled home right now.*

We struggle with the question, What about the Aztecs?
We love them, God loves them even more. He reminds us
that they are His people. Not ours. At this point we do not
know if we will ever go back to live there again, but we
are grateful that He has allowed us these years of ministry
among them. Hopefully another team will be able to com-
plete the Isthmus Nahuatl New Testament for them in
God's own perfect timing."

Even though we sacrificed our earlier dreams of translation work for counseling, it seemed like we made very little
progress. The door to his heart was solidly nailed shut. The
self-help books I read advised letting your partner know what
would please you, since no one can read another person's
mind. So, during one of our retreats, I said I would like him to
be more affectionate and use endearing terms when he talks to
me. His sarcastic reply was, "Well, you just want to be wor-
shipped!" I angrily retorted, "No! I just want to be loved!" I
stormed out of the room sobbing hysterically.

I battled against depression—I couldn't sing anymore
when we went to church. In fact, going to church became a
chore. I toyed with the thought that I would be better off dead
than live like this. But I knew I didn't have the courage to kill
myself. Divorce really wasn't an option, either, because of the
social stigma from family and peers.

Amid this personal despair, I strove to excel in stateside
nursing, even though I had been out of the loop for 10 years. I
took a refresher course in nursing and worked at several staff
nurse jobs: Baylor University Medical Center, Presbyterian
Village retirement center, and as on-call private duty nurse
with Medical Personnel Pool. Getting back into my nursing
career helped me regain self-respect and confidence. Regular
employment helped boost our finances, which were getting
very low. Some of our supporters wrongly assumed that being
assigned in the States meant we got a salary.

In 1978, I accepted an invitation to develop and manage a medical clinic at the linguistic training center. As a full-time volunteer in this new venture, I thoroughly enjoyed being in on the ground floor of this ministry. I arranged for local doctors to give one day each week to diagnose and treat faculty, staff, and students as well as large numbers of our missionary colleagues who passed through the Center on their way to foreign assignments and those returning from other countries with many medical and emotional problems. To minister holistically to our colleagues, I needed to better understand human dynamics so I took psychology courses at Dallas Baptist University and stimulating graduate psychology courses at Texas Women's University. These studies did wonders for my tattered and sagging self-esteem.

CARL

The counseling sessions were intensive, as I knew they would be, so we arranged some weekend getaways at Holly Lake Ranch Condominium, thanks to dear friends. It was there I wrote in my journal,

> Why are we here? To rest. To be free of responsibilities. To focus attention on each other and search each other's soul for better understanding. To enjoy activities together: tennis, swim, hike, play Scrabble, listen to tapes, pray, and study the Word. How can we make the best use of our time here to restore our sexual relationship? We're sleeping in the same bed, but I haven't yet felt free to initiate love-making.

In January 1976, Dr. W. recommended we attend Christian Marriage Encounter. It was meant to be a refreshing weekend of revitalization to our tired, frazzled souls. I was able to open up a bit more as we worked on some of the writing assignments. Initially, I was optimistic that maybe we could work ourselves out of this quagmire. For several months, until summertime, our relationship was more positive and steady, and it felt so good. Even Carolyn, as a teenager, could tell a difference. But those positive experiences didn't last long. I again lost interest when the regular writing assignments became a burden and petered out eventually as winter gave way to spring.

For the next five years I was engrossed and preoccupied with the heavy responsibilities I had for developing typesetting programs for the translated New Testaments our colleagues submitted. I felt much more comfortable in a structured work environment than I had been in our own translation program, which had required someone who is a self-starter. However, that experience in linguistics and translation uniquely qualified me to work in this technical side of Bible Translation. It provided me with a lot of satisfaction and sense of accomplishment.

When Dr. W. and his family went back to Guatemala in 1977 to complete their work there, he referred Marilyn and me to another psychologist, Jim E. The two of us continued with Jim for a couple of years. I thought I was making progress so I tried doing without counseling for a year, more or less coasting along.

My journal entries in March, 1981, reflect some of the growing distress. One entry reads,

> Last night was the time of another one of our marathon talk times—till 1 a.m. this time. I felt pretty good till midnight, then after that it got depressing. Marilyn said she would be relieved if I decided to end the marriage. She sounded like she really meant it. She wants a man that likes women. And she would like to meet and shake hands with any woman who would take me on!

A second entry that year reads,

> The desire to be liked, to have a buddy, maybe even to be that other person, is neurotic. This need seems

to be as much a part of me as my right hand. It is one of those childish things that must be put away. The sexual energy tied in with that need makes a powerful but deceitful package. I haven't yet convinced myself that pursuing the fulfillment of this need is absolutely unprofitable, futile, and self-defeating.

We've tried so hard to make it work. If we give up now, we will wonder if we should have given up years ago and saved ourselves all this heartache. I do not enjoy Marilyn's companionship these days. I'm sorry, Marilyn. I know you miss mine. I see your anguish. I cry for you. I remember your words, "You just try to see how far you can push me away from you!"

My moods fluctuated and my attitude toward women remained one of contempt and resentment. In 1980 I was faced with increasingly devious and troublesome thinking patterns that I could no longer deny. My behavior became more erratic, deviant, and irrational. Desperate, I began therapy again, this time with Larry, another psychologist. One evening, after a session with Larry, I got into some real pain: *I'm crying for the child I never was. I'm saying goodbye. I don't want to grow up. I'm not ready yet. I haven't finished being a boy. I never get enough. One parent says Stay Little. Another says Grow Up. I get mixed signals. I'm torn between them. I stay little but try to grow up.*

All through that spring and summer I continued sessions with Larry. This came up in group one evening: *"Momma, I need you to tell me I'm okay, to know that you love me. There must be something wrong with me. You don't love me.*

The stress of the hard work with Larry began to bring up the familiar anxieties. When summer came, with scantily clad people out in public view, it became harder for me to rein in my thoughts and fantasies about nudity and same-sex attractions. It wasn't long until I was back to the same pattern: moodiness, isolation, secretiveness, non-communication with my family.

A May 10 journal entry reads,

I worked on feelings for awhile in my room. Reached some pain around mother's discomfort with talking about God and prayer. Told her she made it hard for me to talk about God, prayer, deep personal things. It was hard to say that. I choked up, crying. One truth stood out: I couldn't be me and please Mother. As a child I tried to please her but only managed to stifle myself. I bitterly resented her for this.

As a child, one way I symbolized my freedom was to take off my clothes when mom and dad weren't around. I was reminded of that today as Marilyn pulled out of the garage and the doors closed. I felt compelled to take off my clothes and go around the house naked. My resentment over being stifled and not daring to be me was involved in the scene at the altar one night at revival meeting. I quit praying as soon as I saw mother up there kneeling in front of me. I needed to break loose. I needed to be me. I needed to be free. But I wasn't ready to assert that prerogative in her presence. I viewed her as not being free, and so therefore, I didn't dare be free.

At Larry's suggestion, I began what was then called Primal Therapy, a week-end of intensive therapy that used guided imagery to delve into the psyche, even prenatal experiences, through mild hypnosis-type sessions. As he gently guided me, I uncovered some infant and early childhood fears that he strongly believed have caused my emotional development to be stunted or arrested. This, in turn, has prevented me from making the best use of the therapy we've had over the years. The sessions were exhausting, but as a fifty-year-old man, desperate to uproot and understand my sexual hang ups, I stuck with it for the entire time.

MARILYN

Where do I fit into all of Carl's work with Larry and the primal therapy, I wondered? He rarely shared anything with me when he returned home from these intense sessions. I felt left out, very vulnerable, anxious, and easily irritated. I worked hard to avoid brooding and depression. The psychology and counseling courses I was taking were good therapy for me.

On November 16, 1980, I received a letter that eased my anxiety to a certain extent. Dr. G., the primal therapist, wrote:

> *Dear Marilyn, at times during the weekend I wished you were here so that I could encourage you along with Carl concerning my optimism with his progress . . . I will write you a note to give you my viewpoint of the therapy.*
>
> *Carl seemed to be closed down with me at first. After a short time, he began moving and the results were very positive . . . from the intensity of it, I tend to believe that his problem will dissolve by itself, though not overnight.*
>
> *I have no idea what your fears, apprehensions, or anxieties are . . . you have your own universe of them. It might help to know this type of problem is not sexual per se, nor is it a moral problem . . . it can be both . . . it goes deep into parental relationships. We have been able to locate specific pain areas dealing with the parents so I am most optimistic that Carl's problem will be corrected soon. I encourage you to be patient and supportive, as I know you have been. God is at work and He will perfect that which He has begun. Yours in Christian concern. Dr. G.*

With Carl so absorbed with his own personal struggles, he was minimally involved with our daughter's need for fatherly guidance. Her first year in college she met Mark, and six weeks later they called us to tell us they wanted to spend the rest of their lives together and asked for our blessing on their engagement. Congruent with his lack of parental involvement, Carl said, "Oh sure!" Much *too* readily, I thought. Did he just want to absolve himself completely of parental responsibility? I had hoped they would get to know each other better and take more time to think about such a momentous decision. They were married eight months later at the end of that school year, May 30, 1980.

Six days after the wedding, I needed surgery for a hysterectomy. I hoped this would improve our chances of intimacy without the monthly interruptions, which he said grossed him out. We could be more relaxed and decrease some tension. But nothing changed. If anything, my attempts to initiate lovemaking were rejected more than usual. His sexual fantasies about other men held great power over him and I couldn't compete with that.

By March 1981, I was emotionally drained, so I backed off for a week to reflect and to take a break from his long silences, moodiness, and irritability. A friend offered me her cozy cottage for that week. I chose not to tell Carl where I was—but I did give him the phone number. He was upset when he discovered he had to fend for himself without knowing where I was! During that week, for the first time, I saw myself as a person separate from him, responsible for my own issues and feelings. This time of reflection launched my sense of self-empowerment. In August 1981, I graduated *magna cum laude* from Dallas Baptist University with a degree in psychology and counseling—a big milestone and accomplishment. Now I felt more in charge of my life and less dependent on our relationship for satisfaction.

This joy was soon dulled a few days later when, as I hunted for something on his office desk, I found graphic and detailed notes about his same-sex fantasies. Hurt and rage boiled up inside me. I either needed to kick him out or move out myself. Having begun to detach emotionally from him, I rented an apartment in North Dallas and drove back and forth to my work at the clinic. During this time apart, I honestly faced myself. How much more pain and hurt could I tolerate? It's a good thing I didn't know what mental anguish was ahead or who knows what I might have done. Small doses at a time probably prevented me from going to pieces entirely or doing something more drastic. My life was unfolding in some unexpected ways. I was thankful I could rely on friends' support and my faith in God.

That faith was deeply tested when my suspicions that Carl was acting out his fantasies proved to be true. In September I discovered more notes—his description of a same-sex encounter he had in a gay bath. When I confronted him, he admitted that he had frequented gay bars, attended the Metropolitan Community Church for gay people, and even joined Club Dallas for gays. He said he was totally clueless about what he needed to do to overcome the strong pull he had toward the homosexual lifestyle. He didn't seem to be aware of what it did to our relationship—little guilt or pangs of conscience.

I was crushed all over again, just as I was hoping to extricate myself from all this pain. If, after all the counseling we'd had he still chose this lifestyle, then so be it. He was self-willed and determined to do what he wanted to do, hiding behind the marriage and causing me great pain. I had fought long and hard enough, I felt. There was nothing more for me to do except to end the relationship. So even though it went against everything I believed in, I filed for divorce in September 1981. That afternoon I called our pastor and his wife and they invited me to their home where I poured out my pain. Jackie held me tight and rubbed my arms and back until I calmed down. After he was served the divorce papers later that day, Carl moved out of the house. I thought I was ready to let go, but years of co-dependent, tug-of-war, push-pull, approach-avoidance interactions didn't go away instantly. I wasn't convinced I had the courage to go through with the divorce after the required sixty-day waiting period.

Despite my personal anguish, at some level I felt compassion for Carl who was in the grips of his own mental and emotional torture. Part of me wanted to be optimistic that he could work through this phase. Was he having a midlife crisis of some sort? A bigger part of me wanted to run as far away as I could from this person that I didn't know anymore. I asked him one day what he would do if he was divorced and living all alone. He said, "I would probably be promiscuous." At a time when HIV/AIDS was emerging, was that a reason to stay in the marriage—to protect him from such a fate? My heart yo-yoed back and forth, but it was clear to me that he had progressed very little beyond the emotional immaturity the psychiatrist used as a reason to reject him from military service thirty years earlier.

Even though a mixture of pain and grief haunted me, the medical work at the clinic continued to give me much satisfaction. I wanted to continue membership in the mission even if I was divorced. I couldn't bear the thought of leaving the closest family/friends I had. This had been my family for twenty years. However, mission policy wouldn't allow a person who had initiated divorce to remain as a full member. If I went through with it, I would have to resign. They said I could later reapply as a "short-term assistant." Several colleagues wrote letters to the board advocating on my behalf, assuring the board that I was not at fault in the marriage. The board wouldn't budge on the basis of "policy."

Where was God? Hadn't he called us to share his word with people who had no Bible in their language? Would he ever allow us to return to our translation work in Mexico? I was torn between trusting and questioning him. In December 1981, I reluctantly resigned from the mission—the hardest thing I have ever done. It felt like I'd been thrown overboard and left to drift and drown on a stormy sea. It was impossible to make sense of this immense loss. Besides losing a twenty-seven-year marriage, I was losing my Wycliffe family, too.

By now, word had spread to our colleagues about the reason for the break-up of our marriage. How judgmental would they be? This would probably verify who my real friends were. Gossip about other members who had divorced or committed similar indiscretions was fresh in my mind. Even my parents expressed extreme disapproval of my decision to file for divorce. They had little understanding of what I faced. I had to depend more than ever on God's strength and guidance through these rough waters.

When the end of the sixty-day waiting period came, I couldn't cut the marriage ties. Carl expressed relief when I told him that I had decided not to go through with the divorce. He said maybe now we could work on our relationship in new and creative ways since he felt he was gaining confidence and ability to change his thinking. He assured me that he really could make the necessary changes.

We discussed reasons for staying together and doing the best we could: neither of us wanted to grow old alone; we shared a daughter, son in law, and five lovely grandchildren; we could aim at companionship and celibacy—"just being friends"; we had hobbies and other interests in common; divorce would just exchange one set of problems for another. We had looked into the abyss of divorce and didn't like what we saw. Both of us wanted to make this work.

Late in December 1981 we agreed to rent our house to students and move to an apartment in Richardson, convenient to Carl's new employment. I took a staff nurse position at Richardson Medical Center. From this point on, it was uncharted emotional territory, fraught with uncertainty and fragile connections. It was a wild and emotionally stormy ride as we roller-coasted through this marital turmoil. I truly wanted to believe Carl was sincere and that he deserved another chance. After all, no one is perfect.

He seemed to have a more repentant attitude and said he was recommitting to not pursue the gay lifestyle. As he began to share aspects of his spiritual journey more openly with me, my anger dissipated to some extent. Despite his charm and reassurances, I wasn't sure I could trust him to maintain any of this in a sustained way. He was good at manipulation. Trust had become a real issue with me—and it still is. I was committed to doing my part but, because he vacillated so much, it was difficult for me to believe that he was truly committed to change his ways.

As spring turned into summer he found it hard to control his same-sex attractions, moods, and thinking patterns. Lounging around the apartment pool during the scorching hot Texas weather provided lots of near-naked bodies for him to fantasize about. So here we were back to square one again—his unpredictable moods took over. I was left in the lurch as he regressed despite his good intentions. He confessed to having a wandering, lustful eye, always looking for that perfect male body that appealed to him. Even out in public, when we went to a nice restaurant, he ogled someone across the room instead of enjoying my company. Nothing had really changed.

I began to recognize this as an addictive pattern that was not going to go away easily. A friend suggested I attend Al-Anon meetings. It was helpful to recognize how I *allow* myself to be battered emotionally—a new thought for me. I needed to pull away from him again. In August I rented a room near my work at the hospital. It was a relief from the tense, strained relationship. I could go to work with a lighter heart.

Ironically, he was more attentive to me from a distance. He called me frequently to suggest we do something together. It was obvious he could love and appreciate me at a distance when closeness and intimacy weren't possible or expected. It put me at a distinct disadvantage to know how to cope with his ambivalence. It was as if he wanted it both ways—at some level he was dependent on me for friendship but yet wanted to hang on to his fantasy life.

We lived separately for three months. I started attending a therapy group and keeping a journal to help me sort through murky issues. I asked myself, Why would I stay married to him? My response went something like this: He is a person with a lot of potential; I want to help him develop that potential; he is the father of our children; I didn't want the pain of divorce and an uncertain future. He was a wonderful "fix-it" man, talented and skillful in many ways.

What did I want for the future? I wanted us to have open, honest communication; to love unconditionally and be non-defensive; to have each other's welfare in mind and desire the best for each other; to give each other frequent compliments; to accept the aging process together; to have loving spirits and to be devoted companions, to take classes together, to learn a sport together; to give each other space and not attempt to control the other.

CARL

When my supervisor at the Wycliffe Center learned about my moral lapse, I was asked to resign from the mission immediately. After the divorce papers were served, we just exchanged living quarters. I packed up my stuff and moved to the apartment Marilyn had rented in North Dallas and she moved her stuff back to our home. Job-hunting was not easy, but I was fortunate to land a good job in my field of expertise—computer-assisted typesetting.

Being confronted with divorce was a wake-up call for me, since I was so strongly opposed to it. I realized then my behaviors and attitudes were irrational. The drastic consequences of being unfaithful to my spouse had never occurred to me before. The "love" I professed to have did not include empathy and nurture. Instead, I was indifferent and contemptuous of a woman's needs. I thought about how lonely and frustrated Marilyn has been all these years. I thought about my own confused and conflicted feelings. Where do I go with all this?

In my despair I asked a couple of trusted friends to help me sort out my spiritual conflicts. Was there hope for any turn-around? If there was even a smidgen of hope, I prayed I would find it. During the next two months, I met with a small group of friends who ministered to people who truly desired to give up the homosexual lifestyle. I struggled to gain a better understanding of the power of temptation as well as my addictive thought processes and behavior. Down deep, I believed that the gay lifestyle was not a satisfying way to live; it degrades all persons involved.

I wrote to Marilyn before she moved out. The letter read,

> *"Tomorrow you're leaving. I am sorry it has come to this, but I see that it is best not to allow an intolerable situation to go on endlessly. We have said about everything that can be said, I suppose, but I want to write a few things down. I was thinking today how supportive you have been to all of my higher aspirations and goals—everything I have set my heart to doing. I really appreciate that. It's certainly a plus quality that you bring to our relationship. It is a quality that will encourage me when or if we become husband and wife—really and truly.*
>
> *When I think about the pain I have caused you, I hurt inside. You didn't do anything to deserve all that. And now seeing you face the uprooting that goes with leaving a place that you wanted to call home with me—it feels like a heavy load on my heart. I want to cry out, "Don't go! Please! I'll love and protect you. We're part of each other. It's not right. It's not fair." But with tears I must admit that it's even less fair to keep raising your hopes only to have them dashed again. And it just tears me up to realize that I can't promise the same thing wouldn't continue to happen again and again if you stay. I will do whatever is in my power to let people know that our separation is not due to any wrong-doing on your part or that I blame you for it.*

I missed Marilyn but I longed for an end to the difficult, confused mixture of feelings I was experiencing. I met with two Christian married men who were also gay and struggled over similar issues with their wives. One might say it was mutual commiseration rather than support. Eventually both of them divorced their spouses.

Chapter 8

Navigating Through Rough Waters:
Our Garland, Texas Home
December 1982–December 1987

MARILYN

Eighteen months earlier we sold some rental property. Now was our last chance to invest the money to avoid capital gains tax. What better way to invest the proceeds than to buy another house? That raised the issue of whether we were ready to live together again. We tentatively started looking at houses on our days off. That was enough to revive our flagging spirits and stimulate our creativity! Plans and dreams of owning a new home infused our relationship with added sparkle! Still living separately, though, during that time, we worked on our issues with a therapist and group process. Three-and-a-half months later, we bought a recently built home in a new development in Garland, a suburb of Dallas, and moved in the week before the Christmas holidays with renewed commitment and optimism.

For the first time in our nearly thirty years of marriage, we eagerly plunged into the excitement, fun, and hard work that goes with living in a brand-new house. We landscaped the outside, constructed a free-standing fireplace for cozy fireside chats and to save on heating bills, decorated inside, planted a large garden, and made the acquaintance of our friendly neighbors. Finally we had the house the way we wanted it! For the next year and a half, as we focused on feathering our nest, we experienced some improvement in our relationship. It was a welcome change to focus on possibilities rather than problems.

Due to the newness of this adventure, we were able to weather the first summer in our new home without any major disruptions. Maybe, I thought, at last we've hit on something positive. But, alas, as the second spring merged into summer, those familiar, troublesome patterns began to emerge. The cycles of fantasizing, distance, silence, and uneasiness reared their ugly heads. Carl sought advice from the pastor of the church we attended but he couldn't seem to shake himself off dead-center. We each continued with our own therapist to help us untangle this complicated web. The advice both of them gave us was: "First resolve the inner-child issues that you each brought to the relationship before you work on marital issues."

My awakening and eventual escape from being an enabler and co-dependent partner began in a therapy group that focused on the book *Women Who Love Too Much: When You Keep Wishing and Hoping He Will Change*, by Robin Norwood. As I joined the group discussion, I learned just how much I was tied in with "people-pleasing" to be accepted and loved. I literally had become an "over-functioner"; this meant my partner had to become an "under-functioner." I began taking steps to break that pattern of trying to control or change our relationship.

Another helpful book was *How to Break Your Addiction to a Person*, by Howard M. Halpern, Ph.D. He advised: "You can't change another person, you can only change yourself." I realized I kept telling myself that if I would just try harder, things would work out. This book helped me identify unhealthy patterns I had developed over the years. I slowly recovered from the toxic pattern of focusing on someone else's behavior when I needed to pay more attention to my own. A July 1985 journal entry reflects some of my new insight:

> I went with my friend Betty to Al-Anon (non-smoking) to see what I could learn about relationships with someone who has a sexual addiction. I must take re-

sponsibility for changing my attitudes and behaviors that have contributed to our dysfunctional relationship.

Co-dependency is a concept that the therapy group helped me explore. I began to see how the emotional baggage I brought to the marriage had been a negative factor, such as feelings of abandonment after my birth mother died, feeling rejection from my stepmother, and my efforts to gain love and acceptance from a man who was emotionally unavailable. The 12-Step group taught me about the futility of doing the same thing over and over but expecting different results. This is the definition of insanity! I kept extensive journals as I learned to accept and nurture myself instead of expecting this from Carl. I stopped trying so hard to please him at the expense of my own individuality. As I put some of the pieces together and practiced these principles, I stopped focusing so intently on Carl and his problems. It changed how I related to him in over-functioning ways. As I discovered who I was apart from him, I was able to express myself more freely.

He was understandably shocked and upset that I had pulled a comfortable rug out from under him, especially as I emotionally distanced myself. If I wasn't "taking care of him" by fussing about and focusing on him, he would have to take care of himself. He was a big boy now and could figure out for himself what he needed to do!

New levels of insight and emotional detachment came with the support of the therapist and the group, and I could be more objective. There was really no need to shed more tears over this ambivalent man in my life. I told myself, *I've cried all the tears I'm going to. He's not worth crying over anymore. I'm a worthwhile person and need to develop stronger personal boundaries.* Occasionally, though, when his rejection overwhelmed me, I still cried silently to myself.

Intimacy was iffy—IF and when *he* wanted it. If he knew I prepared myself for intimacy, e.g. bathing and perfuming my body or donning a sexy night gown, he would begin to perspire despite my attempts to be reassuring. We often played this silly little game: As I crawled in bed, I intentionally turned away from him and pretended I wanted to go to sleep. Then he might initiate lovemaking. He wanted sex without intimacy or emotional attachment.

One time he asked me if I felt I was being "used." I wasn't sure what he meant, so I said, "I don't know." Then he proceeded to tell me that he could only make love by fantasizing about some other male with whom he was infatuated. His narcissism and self-focus was too much for me—he didn't really want *me* as a sexual partner, it was just that I was convenient. Consequently, I became uninterested in being intimate.

Carl worked day shift at the print shop, and I worked evening shift at the hospital. In this way, we each created our own space and rarely interacted. This minimized some tension. If we had something to say to each other, we left notes on the kitchen table. I took quilting lessons and played tennis with friends. He took dancing lessons to find out if he could foster an interest in women. He stayed with it only a few weeks. In addition to being clumsy, he said it involved too much closeness to a female person. Gardening was about the only activity we enjoyed doing together on weekends. The weather in Texas was conducive to a year-round garden. It was satisfying to plant, harvest, and preserve sweet corn, tomatoes, cucumber pickles, and other vegetables, just like when I grew up on the farm.

In August 1987, events took a different turn. Our relationship was at the breaking point again. It was time to re-evaluate our situation. I accepted the offer of a staff nurse position at a mental health facility in Kansas located thirty miles from where our daughter and her family lived and sixty miles from my elderly parents. The 500-mile trip from Texas to visit our family was getting too long and tiresome so this decision was fairly easy. It made it convenient to visit my parents and the grandchildren.

I moved into a small but comfortable apartment near my job. For the next six months starting a new job absorbed all my thoughts and energy. Since Carl stayed in Texas, we occasionally wrote letters and talked infrequently by phone.

CARL

I needed to work another six months to be fully vested in my retirement plan. I was very ambivalent about moving to Kansas and living together. Nothing either of us did seemed to improve our relationship. We put our house in Garland up for sale but homes weren't selling. In the meantime, I tried to figure out what I really wanted out of this relationship.

On August 27, 1987, I wrote to Marilyn after she moved away,

> *I need to deal with the ambivalence that has been so characteristic of my attitude toward you. It's important to find an answer before we attempt to make it together again. I don't have any desire to return to those many heavy-duty conversations. It is certainly different being here alone than when you were away for just a week or so. I miss you a lot. I'm reminding myself, though, that I need to make some real changes in order for us to live together in harmony."*

On September 20, 1987, I wrote her again:

> *After our phone conversation yesterday I had a pretty rough night. It's strange how, despite the oppressive pall that hangs over us, the thought of divorce is extremely painful. . . . The Lord is dealing with me about avoidance and procrastination. As I read over my journal for the past year, I'm reminded of the ways I allow this pattern to continue. One of those areas is the pile-up on my desk. Another pattern is not acknowledging troublesome situations when I'm stimulated visually by some good-looking guy. For example, when we walked in the mall,*

or when we strolled down Bourbon Street in New Orleans or when I was attracted to the photographer who took our pictures. Those would have been ideal times to deal with the issue of my wandering eye and boy-watching habit.

But this avoidance pattern—is there an underlying attitude that must be dealt with first, some seed of defiance that I haven't repented of? The verse from the promise box this morning was Psalm 25:9—'The meek he will guide in judgment, and the meek he will teach his way.'— That's God's promise, and I can only conclude that if I continue to feel perplexed, lost, alone, or clueless, it likely has something to do with defiance and/or pride.

A week later, still ambivalent, I wrote,

I've been thinking about our phone conversation ten days ago. I share your desire to end this unhappy way of relating, and I am seriously weighing divorce—would it be best for all concerned? I'm not convinced that divorce is the way to go. I'm keeping calm, not doing anything rash. Maybe one of your concerns is that I'll get involved with someone. Not to worry. I'm hoping we'll be able to settle the issue when we have a chance to talk again.

I needed something to help me get unstuck in these unhealthy habits and ways of thinking. My therapist believed I was depressed enough to be hospitalized, but for some reason that didn't happen. I acknowledge my long-standing problems with inertia, passivity, and procrastination. I face difficult tasks and relationship issues by conveniently ignoring them. If I put off even relatively minor tasks such as cleaning off my desk and filing important papers, strong feelings of guilt and depression are triggered. These lead me into downward spirals of sexual fantasies and compulsive masturbation, just as others use drugs, alcohol, food, or any compulsive behavior, to dull the pain and guilt feelings.

MARILYN

Two months went by. My letter to Carl went like this

I want to be honest with you. The emotional distance between us shows how effectively you shut me out of your life. When you avoid discussing issues or when we move toward sexual intimacy you become defensive and/or anxious. As a result, I feel emotionally abandoned, used, abused, and in a no-win situation. You control this relationship by being emotionally unavailable, silent, ambivalent, remote, vague, non-committal, and evasive.

Why keep up the facade? Be honest! Don't use me as a substitute for your sexual fantasies! Don't hide behind this marriage simply because it's convenient, cheaper, socially acceptable, or because you fear God's and parents' disapproval. God is not pleased with our marriage the way it is, so there's no reason to feel guilty over a divorce. It's time to stop torturing ourselves.

Take charge, free both of us to get on with our lives, what's left of them! The kindest, most loving thing you can do is to initiate and follow through with divorce proceedings. That's how you can show that you are concerned for my welfare. We both deserve relief from the pain of pretending to be married.

You've said before, "I'm not happy alone and I'm not happy in this relationship.' If you're unhappy alone, then that's your choice and you have only yourself to blame for your misery. You have no right to inflict your discontent on someone else and be insensitive to how it affects another person. On the other hand, I have a right to not be used, abused, abandoned, or discounted by a husband who avoids intimacy or responds reluctantly and grudgingly."

Later I wrote in my journal,

On the phone tonight, Carl says that he wants to hang a "welcome" sign on every room of his life to be more transparent. But he rarely follows through on what he says he will do, especially if it involves effort, discomfort, thinking differently, self-disclosure, or self-discipline. He tells me things he thinks I want to hear. . . . It is clear to me that he is not wholeheartedly invested in this relationship. He has said on several occasions, "I realize that I have a deep need to be taken care of." So I shouldn't be surprised when he resists giving anything in return and alienates anyone who would expect an emotional response from him.

My journal continued,

All along I have hoped for a loving, committed and mutually up-building relationship between us. That's what has kept me hanging in here. Now I am in the process of giving up those hopes. It's taken me a long time to face the reality that I can't compete with the young, attractive males he obsesses about. It is an exercise in futility to hope for un-ambivalent affection from him. His secret thought life is his priority and he jealously guards his privacy. Recently he stated that much of his anger is because he can't have it both ways, which means he wants both a male lover and a woman's nurturing. Well, maybe some other woman can tolerate that emotional yo-yo but not this woman! Not anymore. I consider it an insult to my personhood.

  I am also letting go of hopes that he can ever love the whole person I am—to look beyond outward appearance. I am well aware of my flaws. I am not the most beautiful, best-dressed, slimmest person that would meet his specifications of a perfect body. As age takes its toll, it's not going to get any better. So if his satisfaction depends on the externals, then he'd better think seriously about divorce. His critical attitude toward my body type degrades me and batters my self-confidence. It's hard to maintain my self-esteem and avoid depression when he is dissatisfied, especially as it relates to my surgical scars, weight, and the aging process.

Since I've been living here away from him, it's been a blessed relief not to have that battle. Other people tell me they like me for who I am, so why do I keep fighting his contempt and whims? For me, sex is meaningless without emotional involvement and intimacy. He has said he doesn't want to live the rest of his life without sex. But if he doesn't want the emotional component that is intended to go with it, then it won't do either of us any good. If I can sublimate my desires, he can too. If, by some miracle of God's grace, I maintain a superficial and platonic relationship, sex will cease to be an issue.

So, unless we can negotiate some mutually acceptable agreement, or he can learn to curb his lustful thoughts and wandering eyes, he needs to find someone who doesn't value intimacy or faithful commitment; someone he can toy with but not care about that person's feelings."

During this time of increased awareness about the raw truth of our marriage, I continued to journal by drawing some analogies about how Carl related to me. The first analogy was one of "pet." He wanted a pet, not a partner. A pet doesn't have emotions to consider and doesn't talk back. It is subject to the whims of it owner-master. It is supposed to be there wagging its tail in undying loyalty, but you can kick it away if it becomes too intrusive. It becomes vicious and bites you, however, if kicked too often or ignored too long.

The second analogy was dog in the manger. I was not his type, but he barked so no one else could have me, and stayed in a pretend marriage.

A third analogy described him as a porcupine with quills that kept a mate and others from getting too close. The quills were retractable, however, for periods of time—long enough for him to turn on the charm and create a Mr. Nice Guy image.

A fourth analogy used the image of an iceberg. On the surface he showed the tip of benign, inauspicious appearance and Mr. Nice Guy behavior, but he was treacherous and dangerous underneath—he was unreliable, unpredictable and couldn't't be trusted.

Thanksgiving weekend I visited my friends in Texas I missed greatly. The first night I stayed in our house with Carl. We talked till midnight. He admitted he still has serious doubts about whether he wants to stay married because his attractions are elsewhere. When he said that, I angrily threw my wedding ring at him. "Good riddance," I said, "you need to terminate this crazy-quilt pattern of guilt, shame, dishonesty, doubts, gaminess, ambivalence, and emotional confusion." The tension was high and it was an explosive scene—I couldn't sleep that night. The rest of my time there I stayed at a friend's house and didn't see him again.

As the holidays came around, he was still wrestling with his inner conflicts and said he wanted to spend Christmas Day by himself instead of coming to be with our family. Fine! I accepted that he had to make his own choices. It felt strange, though, for him not to spend Christmas with me, my parents, our children, and grandchildren over the holiday but I discovered I could have a wonderful time without him. The next day he called to tell me that we have a buyer for the house and they want to take possession in a week! So he scurried around, had a garage sale New Year's Day and one of our dear friends helped him pack things that were left for storage.

Chapter 9

WE WALK THROUGH THE FIRE
January 1988–May 1996

CARL

After the house sold and the new occupants moved in, I rented a motel room temporarily until I could make up my mind about what I wanted to do. After Marilyn moved to Kansas it was an unsettled time for me—I was still very ambivalent. I couldn't decide whether I wanted to stay in Texas or live with Marilyn again. I was closer to considering divorce than at any other time.

After many telephone conversations between us, I concluded that I wasn't ready to give up on marriage yet. My journal entry on January 28, 1988, read,

> This evening I told Marilyn I am willing to give it another try—ready to set the pace for change in our relationship. I am ready to make changes with God's direction and help. Psalm 121 reads, "My help comes from the Lord, who made heaven and earth." Taking the initiative would be a major change for me. Given my personality quirks, neither of us is sure that's a realistic expectation. We agreed on the goal of a periodic check-in to evaluate how it's going with us.

So it was that, a week later on a snowy, icy, windy day, I emptied the storage bin, packed a U-Haul with our stuff and drove from Texas to Kansas—prepared to give another effort to live together in the attractive duplex apartment that she had rented.

Marilyn wanted accountability more than I did and proposed the idea of writing up a covenant. We drafted this document and worked on following the guidelines, muddling through until it was obvious I was not honoring our covenant. We tucked it away in the file where it remains today.

It proved too perplexing, confusing, complicated, and demanding for me. I felt coerced, boxed in, and unmotivated to follow through on any commitment. I still couldn't set goals, take responsibility, and commit to action. To be accountable for my attitudes and behavior was a foreign concept to me. My passivity created a vacuum that forced her to take the lead in financial and family matters, recreation, and social activities. I managed to avoid controversial subjects at all cost.

Marilyn could sense when I was preoccupied and distant from her. When she brought up sensitive issues that I didn't want to talk about, I gave her the silent treatment for several days. Other times we talked into the wee hours of the morning trying to identify the barriers to solving these prickly problems, which were mainly due to my self-focus and failure to comprehend the complexities of human relationships. She pleaded with me to be more honest and open. Sometimes I flew into a rage that frightened her to the point that she got into the car and drove away.

Despite my good intentions, the idea of changing my attitude toward her was much too threatening for me. True to my pattern to ease my anxiety, I continued to drift into lustful thoughts, masturbation, and exhibitionistic tendencies. What little intimacy we had before was long gone. I did keep one promise I made: I no longer actively sought same-sex liaisons. I maintained an active fantasy life, however, which proved to be just as damaging to our relationship.

For awhile I met weekly with the healing prayer team, a small group from the church we attended. I shared some of my deeply painful childhood memories. I desperately wanted to experience what was called healing of the memories. Often, when my parents imposed their will on me, I suppressed my anger and harbored resentments against them. I resented Marilyn, too, as a surrogate parental figure. I hated the thought of being a child, but yet at some level, I knew I was acting like one. This mindset kept me firmly stuck in my unhealthy habits, thoughts, and attitudes.

We lived close to a sparsely populated country road. Frequently, when I experienced the compulsion to expose myself, I went over there and did so. When I casually mentioned this to Marilyn, she was genuinely alarmed that I would use such poor judgment and risk arrest. She urged me to seek help in the treatment program for sex offenders at the mental health center where she worked.

I agreed to a psychiatric evaluation and outpatient treatment was recommended. Though I had not been legally charged with anything, I had to acknowledge that I battled the same powerful, addictive urges that could eventually lead me to criminal acting out. A therapist who specialized in the complex issues around deviant sexual behavior worked with me on my addictive behaviors in intensive private sessions. I also attended a treatment group for sex addicts and court-ordered sex offenders.

Through all this I would diligently pray and read Scripture and good books on how to work on intimate relationships, but my narcissism (extreme self focus) prevented me from holding on to the concepts long enough to put the ideas into practice. Despite all the therapy I had, I was still so mixed up with inner-child issues that I could not relate intimately to another person.

MARILYN

I was cautious about living together again. Many times before Carl had been persuasive and sincere, assuring me that he would make every effort to straighten out his thinking. And, for short times, he did invest brief bursts of effort. But, each time he weakened and regressed, my resolve to stay married to him wavered. I very much wanted to believe him but my gut level of trust was at an all-time low.

Being in limbo was not for me, so I considered two options. Either we called it quits now and remarried later if and when he ever got his self together; or we lived together, did the best we could, adjusted our expectations of each other, accepted reality, and depended on God's help. I had experienced too many disappointments. It was like being married to an alcoholic who swears up and down he'll never drink or abuse his spouse again.

My responsibility in this situation was to be honest with myself and him; to be assertive when necessary; to be on guard against playing games; to continue appropriate emotional detachment; to adjust my expectations of intimacy; to stay out of the victim role; learn to re-define our relationship as one of friend, companion, and housemate; to set healthy boundaries for myself and to cultivate an attitude of gratitude. The Serenity Prayer was one that I prayed often—for fuller understanding and wisdom to know the difference between what I could change and what I could not change. We both thought we could agree to be civil to each other and be companionable, platonic housemates. So, with that understanding, during a brutal February ice storm, Carl moved our stuff from Texas to Kansas. We were re-arranging our lives again.

The few carefully selected friends who knew our situation had been strongly advising me to end the marriage. They assured me I gave the best years of my life trying to make this work and the chances were slim that he could ever relate to me or anyone else in a satisfying way. Still, I tried to understand what my motives were. I asked myself: why do I feel compelled to keep trying? Was I being a martyr? Was I choosing to stay in this marriage for some subconscious reason? These questions raced through my mind with no definite answers. My marriage vows before God included being faithful in sickness and in health, until death parts us. I could not forget them. I reasoned this way: *If he were physically crippled, a paraplegic or quadriplegic or had some other physical handicap, would I divorce or abandon him?* No, I don't think so. Clearly, he was an emotionally paralyzed cripple. Conscientiously, I couldn't leave him.

In March our 34th wedding anniversary held little meaning for me. There was not much to celebrate. Instead, I drove to Texas to visit my supportive friends. Also, I hadn't had a chance to say goodbye to that wonderful home in Garland so I parked across the street in full view of the house and tearfully wrote, *Goodbye 1013 Lesa Lane. I enjoyed five years with you, but I've moved on. Goodbye Texas. I belong to Kansas now. Fourteen bittersweet years of our marriage were spent here, but I trust that God worked in our lives. Now I put these years to rest and go on to the next phase of my life. Changes are part of life. Nothing stays the same. Only God never changes. He's my rock and strength. He will be with me wherever I go. I need never fear abandonment, betrayal, or disappointment from Him.*

It was hard to sever ties to Texas. I even waited six months to register for Kansas car and driver's licenses. As we settled into our apartment and jobs, I felt the need for some guidelines to deal with our marital problems. A plan like this could help both of us keep on track and provide measurable goals to let us know if we were making any progress. Otherwise, they would simmer, causing friction and distance. I suggested we write a covenant of accountability. He hesitantly agreed it would be a good idea. But he ended up dragging his feet and eventually petered out altogether.

He talked a lot about hope: hoping things between us would get better, hoping he could change his thinking. Hoping. Hoping. Hoping. If he hoped long enough and prayed hard enough, these pesky problems would automatically go away without doing his part of the work. I lost interest in hearing him talk about hope. I wanted action. I told him he could pray all day and all night, but unless he was willing to set specific goals and work on them, nothing would change. He skillfully dodged these conversations. I pushed for direct answers, but he remained vague, even became agitated and angry.

I believe prayer can work wonders. But God wants our cooperation and, since God gave us a will, we must choose to cooperate with him. It puzzled me that someone with his intelligence couldn't apply the basic principles of living in a good relationship. He insisted he had an inalienable right to privacy, that his secret thought life and fantasies wouldn't affect anybody else but they definitely eroded our relationship.

He often said he was afraid it would hurt me if he told me the truth about himself. I said it hurt just as much or more when he was distant and secretive, forcing me to guess what was going on with him. I couldn't be supportive if I didn't know what his struggles were. He was still so angry with his parents and other authority figures from his early childhood, and I was the convenient emotional punching bag. He never physically abused me, although at times he came close to it.

He admitted that he was hiding behind the marriage to protect his image as a missionary and avoid dealing honestly with his sexual preferences. This was a major reason he didn't want a divorce, he said. The pull toward same-sex alliances would be even stronger if he were single. When he told me this, it seemed like the time had come to stop fostering the deception that we were the "ideal couple" in a harmonious relationship. That was when he decided to make a public statement at church, taking the mask off of that image.

After he made this statement I felt uncomfortable being seen together in that church so I began attending another church. I wanted to distance myself from him, and, besides, that church wasn't a good fit for me. It was a relief to have our "secret" out in the open, though. But what would people think of us? Still a people-pleaser, I had more lessons to learn about being authentic. To quell paralyzing depression, I drew on my inner resources and immersed myself in activities that didn't involve Carl.

Our apartment complex at the edge of town had a variety of birds and wildlife, a meandering stream, lots of trees, well-manicured walking paths, wide expanses of grass and flowers. I took daily morning and evening walks to nurture my spirit. My colleagues at work, faithful friends, and family provided an affirming support system. Friends and I enjoyed concerts, dramas, travel, an occasional dinner and movie together. A week-long spiritual retreat at the Benedictine Abbey in Pecos, New Mexico, renewed my spirits. Little did I know this would fortify me for fiery trials yet to come.

We coasted along for over a year. When Carl told me he had been jogging naked in public I was speechless. He acted as if it were no big deal. He said, "Doesn't everybody do this?" Duh! Here I was again—Mother Confessor—a role I hated. I urged him to seek specialized treatment. I was as concerned about myself as about him because I would feel humiliated if he were arrested for this deviant behavior.

Soon after he began treatment, I asked him to tell me what was so repulsive about me that he rejected me sexually. He said my abdominal surgical scars grossed him out and he wanted me to have them sanded down until they were smooth and invisible. Where he got that idea I'll never know. I felt like the wind had been knocked out of me—I could hardly breathe. "You idiot!" I screamed. "Can't you see those scars represent healing! I wouldn't be alive if I hadn't had those emergency surgeries." I was devastated. Those familiar, heavy feelings of not measuring up to his unrealistic standards of bodily perfection surfaced, leaving me depressed and anxious. In his perception I must be damaged goods.

This was a new edge for me. I was tired of this charade. How could I protect myself against his contemptuous attitude? Despite all our efforts, things were getting worse. He asked if we should seriously consider divorce again. I told him *he* must file for divorce this time if he has such a problem living with me. True to his pattern of avoidance, he never followed through. By holding divorce as an undesirable option, though, we kept trying to make it work. I still held on to my vows—"for better or for worse." Could this get any worse? What would be the next bombshell?

There were three big bombshells. First, Carl was laid off at his job with The Typesetter Inc. in Wichita. Desktop publishing was emerging and there was less demand for typesetters. Second, a few days after being laid off, he went to the doctor for an ailment. The doctor noticed several symptoms of Parkinson's disease, a chronic condition that is treatable with medication but not curable. Third, my nursing supervisor expressed concern that my personal problems were affecting my work so I blurted out what I was up against. Right there in her office I crumpled in a flood of tears, hopelessness, and despair. I felt dazed and didn't know what was happening to me.

She called Carl to urge him to move out of our apartment immediately so I wouldn't have to encounter him until I was more stable. She arranged for me to be admitted to the local hospital where I was given medication to calm my hysteria and help me relax enough to sort out my options. Three days of rest and medication in the hospital helped me gain some emotional equilibrium and feel calm enough to return to the apartment.

After recuperating for a week, I went back to work, relaxed and re-energized. I didn't want to have any contact with Carl. What can I say about the next fifteen months that we lived separately? It was a huge relief to have him gone. This separation had a more permanent feel to it. This time I was better able to detach and focus on what I needed to do and stop fretting or obsessing about his problems. I was thankful for my many blessings—a job with a good income, supportive friends, a comfortable place to live. I became more self confident and enjoyed my independence. I even went car shopping and bought a good used car all by myself!

In my work on the chemical dependency team at the hospital I was acutely aware of the addictive process. It finally dawned on me that sexual addiction is what we've been dealing with for over 35 years but none of the counselors we've talked with have ever uncovered it. A person has to recognize and admit powerlessness over an addiction before any healing can begin. No wonder progress was always eluding us!

I was invited to participate in a therapy group for the spouses of the men in the sexual addiction program. At first I was apprehensive but soon discovered it was helpful to know I was not alone in my dilemma. Other women were married to fickle, distant, sexually deviant, and emotionally unavailable men. I had never talked about that part of my life, even to my best friend. I had always carefully guarded the fact that the man I married had same-sex attractions. The therapist helped us to verbalize our fears, to defuse our anger, decide what we needed to do, and how we were going to manage our lives if we chose to say with our mates.

After a month of separation, I wrote to Carl on November 16, 1989,

I'm not going to refer to this as a marriage anymore. This relationship has been on your terms. But for my own growth and development, I want it to be on my terms, at least for awhile, to stop the emotional yo-yo. I no longer want to be at the mercy of your capricious whims, ambivalence, and contemptuous attitude. I'm not as interested in hearing about your new insights as I am in what you are doing with all the insights after you get them. I want to see more action. You remind me of a small child who wants to discover the big wide world, wanders off to explore it only to come back to make sure mother is still there. You take advantage of me by staying in the marriage to make yourself look normal and to be socially acceptable. I need freedom to go in any direction that seems right for me and not be expected to wait for a better life with you. So, until you can sustain a relationship with me that includes mutual affirmation, affection, respect, intimacy, and love, I will severely limit my contact with you. Your rejection of me as an intimate partner represents a tightly closed door. I'm stepping out of the role of waiting to be loved by you; waiting for you to call or write; waiting for you to change your focus; waiting for you to include me in your life; waiting for you to throw a few hopeful crumbs my way that keep me thinking maybe there's something in this relationship for me. I have yet to see evidence that there's a full meal for me where those crumbs come from.

Six weeks went by with no other contact. One day I called him for some information I needed. We talked briefly. It felt strange. Had I healed enough so that I could tolerate occasional casual contact again? As long as we kept the conversation superficial, it was tolerable. I was aware, though, that I had created a tough shell of protection around me. I was learning how to set my own boundaries.

CARL

The phone call from Marilyn's supervisor jolted me into reality. I finally woke up to how serious the situation was and how my behavior was affecting her emotionally. I found a small basement apartment across town and moved in by the time Marilyn was discharged from the hospital three days later.

After four months of job-hunting, I was unsuccessful and my unemployment benefits were running out. So I enrolled in a master's degree program at the local university. Money for school came when a buyer of one of our properties in Texas paid off his note to us in full—seven months before the balloon payment was due. I took this as a gift from the Lord.

At age sixty, it was exhilarating to be back in academic life. It took my mind off of our conflicts and I did well in my classes. However, being around so many young, attractive male students, I was assaulted with those strong, familiar urges and temptations. My resolve to stay in the marriage began to crumble. I even wrote to my parents about my doubt and ambivalence to stay in the marriage and prolong the misery we both feel.

The specialized therapy gradually helped me come to grips with the reality and seriousness of the issues I faced. I discovered that sexuality and spirituality were closely linked. My life-long pattern has been to minimize and/or ignore my desire for same-sex affection by the use of Scripture and prayer, and then pride myself on being so spiritual. For several months I attended meetings in Wichita called "Freedom At Last," a group of Christian men and women who struggled to be free of homosexual attractions. It was helpful only to a certain point. The changes that would be necessary to overcome my same-sex attraction and social deficits were too daunting for me.

This was a tumultuous time as I worked on trying to understand the troubling inner-child issues and the uneven parenting I had in my youth. Since I had difficulty knowing how to nurture a friendship and was awkward in social situations, distance was my protection against too much involvement with any person. At some level, I felt affection for Marilyn as long as I kept her at arm's length. Intimacy in marriage was fraught with intense anxiety for me. Even though I had plenty of sexual desire, I had no clue how to direct it in healthy ways toward an intimate relationship with a woman.

In January I attended a conference in California on spirituality and recovery from sexual addiction, led by a person who was well-known in this field. There the principles were laid out clearly, prayers and anointing for healing and restoration were offered. I experienced freedom in the Spirit. But after I left the conference, I couldn't seem to internalize the benefits long enough to progress from then on. Even as I meditated on Scripture, my intentions seemed to be waning. I reflected on how the

Holy Spirit had filled me and met my need for a sense of being loved. I prayed for an understanding of how I allow myself to drift into a state of sexual fantasy and passivity. I know these characteristics cause me to regress, but I haven't found a way to prevent them from creeping back in. When I confess the lapses and take my place as forgiven and cleansed, I can thank God for the dear, gentle and special person Marilyn is to me.

Growing up as a lonely, self-focused, and isolated child, I hadn't been free to explore relationships. Empathy was a foreign concept to me. As an assignment from the therapy group, I wrote an empathy letter *as if it was from her viewpoint*:

> *I am writing this to tell you how it is for me when your attractions are elsewhere and you reject me—how it was for me when you said, "You're not my type." I felt like a truck hit me. I feel like running as far away from you as I can so that you'll never have a chance to hurt me like that again. I doubt you'll ever be able to really tune in on how hard that was for me to hear. If I'm not your type, then I'm certainly not special to you. And I can't live that way.*
>
> *I have loved you and done my best to encourage you and be a wife and lover to you. I've made myself vulnerable by believing that you love me and by opening myself up to you. I feel betrayed by your lack of interest. I am afraid—afraid of being used. Like I felt when I realized why you wanted those mirrors in our bedroom, so you could watch yourself—not for any emotional and love connection! I'm also afraid of what it would be like for me if you succumbed again to the urge to expose yourself and were arrested.*
>
> *Carl, all this adds up to emotional abuse. If I seem slow to respond and skeptical of the changes happening in your life, it's because I must protect myself. There's nothing I would rather do than to be your wife and lover, if the relationship is mutual. But I won't agree to live together if I continue to be used and abused.*

We continued individual, conjoint, and group therapy as well as a 12-step recovery group. In early 1990, Marilyn and I tested out what we had gained. We either called each other or got together for a meal. Even though we were still on very shaky ground, I took what to me was a big step and invited Marilyn to go with me to a music concert. As long as we stayed superficial during short times together, I could be more relaxed.

At times our commitment wavered. However, we both experienced personal spiritual growth during this time. There was more honest, open communication and gradually the vast emotional Grand Canyon began to narrow. I could view her from a different perspective. "One day at a time" as the saying goes, to be in recovery from a dysfunctional relationship. There are no quick fixes for problems that were generated over many years. By December 1990, after 18 months separation, we were in almost daily contact.

MARILYN

That empathy letter was like a breath of fresh air! Never before had he expressed even a hint of understanding of what it was like for me to be in this marriage. He was finally admitting he used me as a substitute partner.

As he shared more openly with me about his spiritual journey and the benefits of the conference he experienced, I was so glad for him. He seemed to have reached a level of freedom he hadn't had before. I wanted so much to trust that he could hang on to that. It wasn't long, though, before the wind changed and we were back to our decision to just be friends. I was as puzzled as ever and wondered: is it possible that moving back in the same living space with me, where he is keenly reminded that intimacy is lacking, causes him to lose his grip on his good intentions?

We evaluated our living situations. He liked having his own space. I enjoyed my independence. I now understood better and could accept the fact that his issues had very little to do with me. They were there long before he met me. Through many discussions and soul-searching therapy, we concluded our mixed-sexual relationship could not sustain a healthy sex life. My trust was badly damaged and eroded. I resigned myself to a celibate lifestyle. Personal boundaries had become more important to me. The betrayal and emotional battering had taken its toll. I was learning to trust my own intuitions and adjust my expectations in ways that allowed me the freedom to be myself, to enjoy hobbies and group activities.

As we worked on our issues we emerged with some emotional scars and painful memories, but God's direction and faithfulness took us through the fires and psychological minefields of these tumultuous years. I had gained new insights, reflected on old habits, attempted to develop new, healthier ones, accepted and respected our differences, and strove to face our difficulties with new determination..

I officially retired from the mental health center in May 1996. One chapter of our life together ended and another one began. We would soon find out what He wanted us to do besides sit in a rocking chair the rest of our lives.

CARL

Despite the many rough spots, for the most part we were committed to being polite, friendly, courteous, and considerate of each other. By the end of December 1990, we decided we could live together again. Our kids helped me move my stuff back to our apartment. My journal summary reads,

> We are taking a break from intensive counseling. If we haven't learned enough about communicating by now, there is not much hope. It is time to practice what we've learned. I still struggle with anxiety, panic attacks, and guilt feelings in an intimate relationship. We talk openly about wanting to be sexual, but I still shy away from intimacy. Unwelcome, troubling

thoughts and urges prevent me from relating to Marilyn in anything but a superficial way. My ongoing contempt for women triggers my anxiety. Close contact and nurture of another person just don't seem to be possible for me. The secrecy-privacy barrier has not been fully conquered. Passivity and procrastination continue to raise their ugly heads on a regular basis. I struggle off and on with spiritual issues.

It's been two years since I was diagnosed with Parkinson's disease. Medication is helpful in alleviating some of the symptoms and possibly slowing the progression of the illness. So we live life one day at a time, in an attitude of gratitude. Over all, it's been a positive year, and we are thankful for God's faithful provision and guidance.

In addition to my classes at the university, I worked in the Intensive English lab for foreign students, wrote my thesis, and taught English as a Second Language for five hours a week at a local alternative education class. I graduated with a 4.0 grade average and master's degree in liberal studies, majoring in languages. It was a good feeling of accomplishment.

In May 1994 our family and friends held a celebration primarily for my graduation and secondly for our 40th wedding anniversary. We didn't want to focus on an ambivalent marriage since we hadn't come as far in our relationship as we had hoped. But we had reached a certain level of equilibrium to where we weren't teetering quite so perilously on the brink of separation and/or divorce.

The first year after graduation, I taught English and Creative Writing classes at a local community college, grateful to use my skills in public education. The next year I was pleased when two of my professors asked if I would substitute for two of their classes while they took their sabbaticals. One class was The Nature of Language and the other class was Speech Pathology and Phonology designed for speech therapists. As my Parkinson's symptoms worsened, it became too difficult to write on the board, take notes, or use the overhead projector, so in May 1996, I retired from teaching.

Chapter 10

Refined by Fire, the Retirement Years
1996 to the present

MARILYN

We made another move—this time to Abilene, Kansas, into the farming community where I grew up. A large ranch-style house was available that included a huge garden plot, yard work, and maintenance to provide plenty of activity in our retirement. With no structured work schedules to keep us on track, retirement could show up the worst and/or the best in our relationship.

We both like to work with words, so our colleagues in Mexico eagerly took us up on our offer to finish the Nahuatl-Spanish dictionary. We had started this huge project when we first went to Mexico in 1965 by writing words we heard on 3x5 slips of paper then carefully filing them in a shoebox. Carl also wanted to revise a previous edition of the Nahuatl grammar that he had published fifteen years earlier. To do all this, we bought our first computer and printer and connected with the internet so we could use e-mail to communicate with our Nahuatl-speaking language helpers in Mexico. Both of us embraced these challenges with zest and enthusiasm.

Working together allowed us to focus on a meaningful endeavor instead of moaning and groaning about our problems. Over the next three years, we took two month-long field trips to the Nahuatl language area in Mexico to check our work with native speakers. We wanted to be sure everything in the dictionary and grammar was accurate. Also, before publishing the books, we spent several weeks at our mission headquarters in Tucson, Arizona, where professional assistance for linguistic and translation projects was available. There we put the final touches on both the dictionary and grammar. Finally, in 2001, we drove to Alberta, Canada, to deliver the books to the Hursts, who were there on furlough. On their return to Mexico, they shepherded them through the publication and distribution process. It is satisfying to know that both are now being used extensively in the Nahuatl-speaking areas.

Two years after we moved to Abilene, Carl's Parkinson's symptoms became alarmingly pronounced. We thought he might need another level of care in the near future. Instead, he just needed a medication change at the time. However, we knew it was only a matter of time until the medicines might lose their effectiveness entirely and he would need more care than I could provide. With that in mind, in 2001 we investigated retirement facilities that provided nursing care when needed.

Then we auctioned off most of our worldly goods. Two weeks later, we moved to the independent living section of a retirement community—Kidron Bethel Village in North Newton close to where we had lived before. We've made lots of decisions in our lifetime, but choosing to live at Kidron Bethel was our best. Our combined assets assured us of a reasonable income. We hope it is our last move until we make our final one up higher. We connected again with the same church and community friends we had come to love and appreciate.

CARL

While we lived in Abilene, I did not have my usual men's support group, consequently I regressed emotionally. For example, when Marilyn took a two week trip to California with a friend, I thought it would be a good opportunity to probe deeper into why I felt such a strong compulsion to strip naked and exhibit my body. While I was alone in the apartment one

day, I took a video of myself and invited an imaginary audience
to see me naked. As the camera rolled, I dropped my pants,
turned and walked out onto our third-floor balcony. Anyone
down below could see that I was shirtless, but the solid balcony
wall and the flowers in the planter boxes kept everything below
the waist out of view. Still, in my active imagination, my whole
body was visible to the world. (Footnote: The camcorder hasn't
worked since.)

On her return, Marilyn hadn't yet been home ten minutes
when I asked her if I could read my reflections and show her the
video. Even though she was tired from a long day of travel, she
reluctantly agreed to listen to what I wrote but declined to
watch the video. A lengthy, emotionally charged discussion followed. I tried to explain that maybe if I better understood the
urge to expose myself, we could have healthy intimacy again
after all these many years. Even though I don't keep these things
a secret from Marilyn, they still add to her uneasy, distrustful
feelings. I acknowledge these as shortcomings and must be willing to have God remove them and then ask Him to do so. That
is Step Three of the 12 Steps to Recovery.

I later reflected in my journal:

> Since early childhood, I've relished the idea of being
> naked. As a toddler I remember being curious about
> my body and wondered why all this fuss about keep-
> ing my "thing" hidden. Many times during my child-
> hood and youth, I took off my clothes just for the
> pleasure of it. Sometimes I was alone, sometimes with
> other kids. One memory I have when I was about six
> years old is of waking up in the middle of the night,
> getting out of bed in the same room with my parents,
> taking off my pajamas and getting back into bed.
>
> I've come to understand that these behaviors grow
> out of self-focus and self-will. I revert to experiencing
> something I lust for without thinking of the conse-
> quences. This is further evidence I haven't come very

far since my unfaithfulness at a Dallas gay bath in 1981. That happened on a Sunday afternoon, even though on that very day I heard the sermon on Jesus' temptation in the wilderness. I was too self-willed to follow His example.

MARILYN

When he read his reflections to me, I was angry! Being hit with this right after I got back from a delightful twelve-day trip was truly depressing. He was "dumping" on me again. He had promised me earlier that he would not subject me to things like this again when I returned from a trip. He had reported other times he took his clothes off and walked around the apartment naked. This was congruent with what he did as a child when his parents were away. He also admitted that he still masturbated compulsively. That explained why he was often reserved and didn't act glad to see me when I was gone for several days. He feels guilty about his behavior when his inner child decided to assert himself if nobody was watching.

After a fitful sleep, I woke the next morning with a heavy heart. I told him that I'd rather die than live like this—having the fragile equilibrium that I'd been able to achieve turned up-side-down. I knew he needed affirmation in his attempts to resolve these conflicts within himself, but I wasn't sure I was the right person to do that. All this kept me stirred up inside and prevented his relating in an intimate, loving way.

He was willing to commit to a ninety-day abstinence from the exhibitionistic behavior. He said he realized it was escalating and that the chances were high that he would step over the line. As far as I could tell, he wasn't any nearer to understanding why he had these compulsions or how to prevent their taking over.

The next night, as we took a walk in the park, he said he'd given more thought to the abuse he had suffered from his father when he was a little boy. He wanted to talk more about it.

He became tearful as he remembered being stripped of his pants and beaten with a razor strap. He has disliked his father and has not wanted to be like him. I truly ache for him when I realize the suffering he endured as a boy at the hands of his parents.

To survive this latest upheaval and to keep my own sanity, I emotionally distanced myself even farther from him. I could say I emotionally divorced him, if there is such a term. I'm doubtful if I can ever reattach to this man I can't trust. We ended up sleeping in separate rooms.

As time went on he became more unreliable. I could not trust him to follow through on things he said he would do. He kept telling me he wanted to change. I do believe he *wanted* to do that, but the road to overcome addiction is long and hard. He had wasted so much time and multiple opportunities to get serious about it. I was convinced this was just more wishful thinking on his part. With so many years behind us, it would be more difficult now to overcome the unhealthy patterns he had established.

Sometimes when I became depressed and weary of pretending to be happily married and "the ideal couple," my heart ached for relief. If I could be more open about how things really were, it would help me relax and be more authentic. I have feared being judged harshly or criticized for staying in the marriage.

One evening, when several of my close women friends met together, it felt safe to share with them that, before we were married, Carl hadn't been honest with me about the fact that he has strong homosexual attractions. The women were very accepting, supportive, and understanding, just like I had hoped they would be. It felt strange to tell someone besides the few carefully selected friends who I knew wouldn't judge me. Sharing with friends in this way has lifted some of the heaviness from my heart.

It's been very hard for Carl to think of "being real." Even though he's torn up and confused inside much of the time, putting forth a good public image has always been one of his priorities. Until now he has carefully avoided sharing the truth about our relationship, but shortly after I told the women's group, he disclosed his compulsions to the men in his Bible study group. They were also non-judgmental.

Writing about our life in this memoir is another step toward taking off the masks and let others know us for who we are. It has even cleared out some of the tangle of confusion by opening up some long-standing blocks of communication between the two of us. As Parkinson's progresses, my relationship with Carl has evolved into a purely caregiver role. I take each day as it comes and trust God to strengthen me spiritually, physically, and emotionally for whatever is ahead for me.

Channeling my energy into worthwhile projects has been a priority. A rewarding and satisfying part of my retirement has been to help establish a congregational health ministry in our church. We encourage people to maintain a healthy lifestyle, provide transportation to medical appointments, arrange respite care when needed, obtain the necessary information for managing medications and treatments, and stay with members in the hospital, especially those who don't have immediate family nearby. In this way, members who are in the medical and allied health professions are able to support others who attend our church.

CARL

We agreed that companionship and platonic friendship are preferable to the single life so we settled for that. I would not have chosen to live only as friends, but our attempts at being lovers have been fraught with roller-coaster emotions, stress, and crazy-making interactions. I could not relax enough during intimate times to avoid fantasies of making love to someone else with whom I was infatuated.

How would I explain our relationship? If someone were to ask me, "I notice you wear a wedding ring. Why doesn't Marilyn wear one?" what would I say? I have mentally rehearsed an answer: "That's a long story and maybe I'll tell you sometime." Later, I realized wearing that wedding ring was part of the pretense we wanted to give up, so I took it off and put it in safe-keeping.

After we moved back to Newton, I met weekly with several of the same men in the support group at the mental health center where I began in 1989. For reasons as varied as each individual, we needed support to live out our commitment to walk the straight and narrow path in light of addictive sexual behavior.

Despite living with the painful scars in our relationship, I too found ways to channel my energies. I completed an anthology from books I had read over many years. I would recognize something special about a passage and think, *This is good stuff.* I either took it to the computer and typed it out or wrote it long-hand on ruled notebook paper. I worked out a format for presenting the quotes in an interesting and consistent way.

I began composing music and writing lyrics, a hobby that I enjoyed sporadically over the years. I wrote several songs for our church worship services and completed a rather complicated arrangement of a beautiful classical piece by Georges Bizet titled *Intermezzo from Carmen Suite No. 1.* The arrangement includes six or seven instruments that I hope will serve as a church offertory. It was a tedious project, listening to it over and over and separating the instrumental lines. I have passed my music on to the church archives so it can be used in the future.

As Parkinson's has progressed, I have experienced one loss after another. One of the more difficult losses was to give up driving due to slowed reflexes. My computer skills and music hobby were relinquished because I could no longer write legibly or think creatively. Walking has become more difficult and my physical energy is seriously depleted. In January 2008 I was admitted to the nursing wing of the retirement center where we have been living. I am thankful for the good care as I live one day at a time.

CARL AND MARILYN

We will end this memoir with a more positive note. Awesome news came to us in July 2004! We were stunned when the Alumni Director of our *alma mater*, Messiah College, informed us we were chosen to receive the Alumni Distinguished Christian Service Award for the many years we worked in Bible translation among the Aztec people. Our first reaction was shock and awe—a sense of being totally unworthy of such an honor, given the heavy emotional issues that prevented us from completing the work as we had hoped.

We humbly accepted the recognition in a formal ceremony at the alumni banquet. The award was described this way: "This award recognizes outstanding long-term effort in fulfilling the mandates of the Christian gospel to both serve and sacrifice for the needs of humanity."

To be singled out for such an honor was affirming for us and for the Aztec people. We reflected on how God has used our efforts despite our flaws, foibles, and failings. It was heartwarming to acknowledge several of our classmates and fellow-alumni attending the banquet who had supported us through the years with their letters, prayers, and financial gifts. We thank God for letting us have a part in sharing the good news of the gospel. It is important that we praise God for his faithfulness. He uses people like us with all our weaknesses, vulnerabilities, and handicaps to further his Kingdom.

There is another bright spot: The Isthmus Nahuatl New Testament is nearing completion with the dedicated help of capable and enthusiastic Aztec Christians. Chris and Elaine Hurst, the very talented couple we passed the torch to in 1984, have faithfully directed the work we began. It is deeply gratifying to hear reports of new converts and congregations springing up in that area. The handful of Christians, who met in two congregations (with Spanish-speaking preachers) when we started, have grown to an unknown number who meet in fifteen native congregations with Nahuatl-speaking leaders.

They are excited about reading the Scriptures, singing native-authored songs, preaching, and praying in their heart language. We expect to join our Aztec friends and many other language groups singing praises to God around the Throne. Revelation 7:9-10.

Here is a poem Carl wrote recently that reflects on how God has protected us through deep, stormy waters and fiery trials when it would have been so easy to give up:

> After all is said and done,
> And our journey almost run,
> There is one thing left to say,
> God was faithful all the way.

Chapter 11

In Summary

CARL

I am only now beginning to understand how my attitudes and behaviors have poisoned our relationship and made it a non-marriage. I knew from the start of writing this story of our lives that it would either be a whitewash job or a heartrending series of instances that show what it was really like. I should say *is* like because our lives are still being lived. I wanted to be able to say "that was then." But in some ways, *then* is still *now*. Not all the behaviors continue, but some of the attitudes and thinking patterns are all too current. I would welcome a chance to meet all the people to whom I've projected the "ideal couple" image and express my sincere regrets for my hypocrisy.

Until recently, I clung fiercely to the hope that I could learn to ignore same-sex attractions, build up a reservoir of positive, loving feelings, and nurture the heterosexual feelings I did have. I believed that where there is life there is hope. I have finally come to realize that this hope hasn't gone beyond wishful thinking due to my passivity and inertia. I expected change to happen without my active participation.

Recently, the diagnosis of Asperger's Syndrome, a high-functioning form of autism, was offered as a possible explanation for my poor choices, the inability to establish meaningful relationships, and avoidance of marital intimacy. Persons with this diagnosis are often high achievers academically and mechanically but are inept in setting goals and find it difficult to negotiate social situations. This certainly fits with my abilities in mechanical, linguistic, and construction projects. It also accurately describes many of the characteristics that have kept me socially isolated over the years and unable to interact with people in satisfying ways. As we've researched this disorder we understand better why it has been so hard to relate to each other. More information can be found in the DSM IV or at this web address: *www.aspergers.com*

I always thought of myself as a compassionate person but have discovered that I am self-focused and self-willed, with a greatly restricted ability to identify my feelings or empathize with other people's feelings. I find it hard to concentrate on what another person is saying so I miss a lot in conversations.

Over these fifty-plus years my attitude toward Marilyn has been a jumbled mixture of affection and fear, loyalty and disloyalty, love and contempt, attraction and aversion. If I were to counsel others with this degree of ambivalence, I would tell them to decide which side of the fence they wanted to be on and get with the program. I have truly done Marilyn a disservice. First, by not facing reality and telling the truth before we were married; and second, by not giving it my best effort to face the negative baggage, eliminate it straight on after marriage, and nurture the positive traits in each of us.

A nagging question persisted in regard to supporting myself: What kind of job can a linguist/Bible translator find when the avenue has been closed by a moral lapse? I admit financial dependency was a key factor in my decision to avoid divorce. These stresses have been difficult for both of us and Marilyn's willingness to be a caregiver for one such as I is an amazing gift.

MARILYN

This marriage has been a bittersweet experience. We came so close to giving up several times. Writing these reflections has pushed mixed feelings to the surface. This project of intense sharing of ourselves has yielded some unexpected connections for us as we searched for the best way to express ourselves so that it makes sense to someone else.

I have often felt broken and unlovable. Was something wrong with me? Why would a man marry me and not desire intimacy but instead be emotionally unavailable and abusive? Did I subconsciously invite emotional abuse? I don't believe he consciously intended to hurt me, but he was totally clueless as to how his actions and attitudes affected me. If I tried to tell him how they affected me, he ignored or minimized my feelings. His sexual orientation is such a huge barrier to his ability to relate to a woman. Knowing more about Asperger's Syndrome has helped me take it less personally.

Since we chose not to divorce, we carved out the type of relationship that allows us the greatest flexibility and personal spaces. I know for certain that I do not regret my genuine, sincere efforts to be a faithful partner. I have made major adjustments in what I can expect in this relationship. I do not seek anyone's pity but rather understanding and empathy. It is my desire that by taking off the masks to this extent, it will encourage others who may be struggling with *what is* to experience God's faithfulness. My aim is to be truthful, authentic, and straightforward, knowing some readers may perceive me negatively or judge me critically.

At times I feel vulnerable and wonder if I should have gone through with the divorce in 1981. Later, when Carl was so ambivalent about staying in the marriage, would ending the marriage have been preferable? How would our lives have turned out differently? Would each of us have been happy and free to move on—or riddled with guilt because painful issues remained unresolved? That's something we'll never know.

I earnestly hoped and prayed that we could end our journey with a glowing affirmation of married bliss. It was not to be. Even though our story has ended on a rather bleak, matter-of-fact note, there is a positive outcome—I have honored my vows and we are still together. With God's help we have weathered the rough spots.

I am now in the role of caregiver, encouraging Carl to stay as healthy and independent as possible with stimulating activities as his energy allows. He likes crossword puzzles and brief visits with close friends but can no longer travel or be involved in church and community events.

Our type of relationship is not what every couple could settle for, but for us, this is the best outcome. I am finally accepting the fact that when stunted emotions and homosexual orientation are so deeply embedded in a person's psyche, the odds are against change. In order for me not to be hurt again, we both knew we can only be friends, not lovers. That is *what is.* A friend shared a book *Loving What Is,* by Byron Katie with Stephen Mitchell (Three Rivers Press). Even though I haven't come to where I can say I *love what is*, I strive to *accept what is.* During the toughest times, I hold on to this quote by Charlotte Bronte: "I believe in some blending of hope and sunshine sweetening the worst of lots. I believe that this life is not all there is; neither the beginning, nor the end. I believe while I tremble; I trust while I weep."

The insight Virginia Satir expressed at a 1986 Los Angeles meeting of mental health professionals also helped me accept *what is.* Satir stressed that life is what it actually is, not what we wish it to be, but that we are still not left powerless, because "The way in which we respond will direct and influence the event more than the event itself."

Bibliography

A select list of books that have been helpful

Beattie, Melody. *Co-Dependent No More: How to Stop Controlling Others and Start Caring for Yourself.* Center City, Minn.: Hazelden,1987.

——. *Beyond Co-Dependency: and Getting Better all the Time.* San Francisco, Calif.: Harper Hazelden, 1989.

——. *The Language of Letting Go;* Center City, Minn.: Hazelden, 1990.

Byrd, Walter and Marilee Horton. *Keeping Your Balance: A Woman's Guide to Physical, Emotional, and Spiritual Well-Being;* Waco, Tex.: Word Books, 1984.

Halpern, Howard M. *How To Break Your Addiction To a Person.* New York: Bantam Books, 1982.

Katie, Byron. *Loving What Is: Four Questions That Can Change Your Life.* New York: Three Rivers Press, 2002.

Miller, J. Keith. *A Hunger For Healing,* San Francisco, Calif.: Harper Collins, 1991.

Norris, Kathleen. *Dakota: A Spiritual Geography.* Boston New York: Houghton-Mifflin ,1993.

Norwood, Robin. *Women Who Love Too Much: When You Keep Wishing and Hoping He'll Change.* New York: Pocket Press, 1985.

Prather, Hugh and Gail. *The More We Find In Each Other.* New York: Hazelden, 1990.

Robison, John Elder. *Look Me In The Eye: My Life with Asperger's.* New York: Crown Publishers, 2007.

The Authors

Marilyn Wolgemuth grew up during the Great Depression on a Kansas wheat and cattle ranch. After high school, she graduated from Messiah College, Grantham, Pennsylvania, received her RN in Lancaster, Pennsylvania, returned for a BS in Nursing at Messiah College, and earned a BS in Psychology and Counseling at Dallas Baptist University, Dallas, Texas.

She and her husband have one daughter and five adult grandchildren. She has devoted her entire adult life to Christian service, first with Mennonite Central Committee among California agricultural migrants as Fresno County Public Health Nurse, then as a nurse/linguist-translator with Wycliffe Bible Translators and Summer Institute of Linguistics among an indigenous Aztec people group in southern Mexico.

Marilyn has many years of nursing experience, including mental health nursing, and retired in 1996 from Prairie View Mental Health Services in Newton, Kansas. Since retirement, she helped to initiate a parish nurse program in the church they attend, Shalom Mennonite Church in Newton, and is currently one of the parish nurses there. She now lives independently in a retirement center in North Newton.

J. Carl Wolgemuth grew up in Lancaster County, Pennsylvania and graduated from Messiah College with a BA degree in Religious Education. He met Marilyn there and they married in 1954. Together they spent thirteen years in primitive Aztec villages as linguist/translators with Wycliffe Bible Translators. They spent seven years at WBT's International Center, where Carl became proficient in the field of computer-assisted typesetting New Testaments in various indigenous languages.

He furthered his education at Wichita (Kan.) State University, where he graduated in 1994 with a Master's degree in Linguistics, English, and Communicative Disorders and Sciences. He taught Language and Phonetics for two years. He was diagnosed with Parkinson's disease in 1989. Declining health made teaching too difficult, so he retired in 1996. Now being cared for in a healthcare setting, he maintains a keen interest in music, art, and reading science magazines.

CPSIA information can be obtained at www.ICGtesting.com
Printed in the USA
240869LV00003B/1/P